D0417443

# 85

## INSPIRING WAYS TO MARKET YOUR SMALL BUSINESS

*If you want to know how ...*

**100 Ways to Make Your Business a Success**
*A resource book for small business managers*

**The Small Business Start-up Workbook**
*A step-by-step guide to starting the business you've dreamed of*

**How To Get Free Publicity**
*A handbook for small businesses, clubs, schools or charities*

**How To Grow Your Small Business Rapidly Online**
*Cost effective ways of making the internet really work for your business*

**Sale or Succession?**
*How to plan for a successful business exit*

**howto**books

Please send for a free copy of the latest catalogue:

How To Books
Spring Hill House, Spring Hill Road,
Begbroke, Oxford OX5 1RX, United Kingdom
Tel: (01865) 375794. Fax: (01865) 379162.
info@howtobooks.co.uk
www.howtobooks.co.uk

'Inspiring, self-help, marketing strategies that you can apply to your own business **immediately**.'

# 85
# INSPIRING
# WAYS TO
# MARKET
# YOUR SMALL
# BUSINESS
## JACKIE JARVIS

**howto**books

Published by How To Books Ltd
Spring Hill House, Spring Hill Road
Begbroke, Oxford OX5 1RX
Tel: (01865) 375794. Fax: (01865) 379162
info@howtobooks.co.uk
www.howtobooks.co.uk

All rights reserved. No part of this work may be reproduced or stored in an information retrieval
system (other than for purposes of review) without the express permission of the publisher in writing.

The right of Jackie Jarvis to be identified as author of this work has been asserted by her in
accordance with the Copyright, Designs and Patents Act 1988.

© Copyright 2007 Jackie Jarvis

British Library Cataloguing in Publication Data.
A catalogue record for this book is available from the British Library.

ISBN 13: 978 1 84528 167 0

Cover design by Baseline Arts Ltd, Oxford
Produced for How To Books by Deer Park Productions, Tavistock
Typeset by PDQ Typesetting, Newcastle-under-Lyme, Staffs.
Printed and bound in Great Britain by Cromwell Press Ltd, Trowbridge, Wiltshire

NOTE: The material contained in this book is set out in good faith for general guidance and no
liability can be accepted for loss or expense incurred as a result of relying in particular circumstances
on statements made in the book. Laws and regulations are complex and liable to change, and readers
should check the current position with the relevant authorities before making personal arrangements.

# Contents

## Dedication

This book is dedicated to my partner Andrew who, believing in me, has given his complete support and encouragement throughout. Thank you. You are the best.

It is also dedicated to my wonderful horse 'She's Magic': riding her has inspired many of my ideas.

## Acknowledgements

With grateful thanks to my dear friend Julia Clay for her numerous valuable suggestions and comments and dedicated help with proof-reading. Thanks also to my good friend Dan Anderson for his words of encouragement and advice. (I hope seeing this book in print will inspire you to write your book!) A special thank you to my father Roger Jarvis, my grandmother Peggy Jarvis and all of my family and friends for their love and support and continually asking how I was getting on. You all kept me going which I appreciate very much.

## Bibliography

*Getting Everything You Can Out Of All That You Have Got*, Jay Abraham, Piatkus Books, 2001

*Anyone Can Do It – Building the Coffee Republic From Our Kitchen Table*, Sahar and Bobby Hashemi, Capstone Publishing Ltd, 2003

*Quantum Leap* –Robert Clay, Business Growth Workshop; see *www.dspconnect.com*

Cardell Media Website Resources, Chris Cardell, *www.cardellmedia.co.uk*

The following e-books may be found at *www.moneymakingmarketingideas.com*: (in our recommended e-books section).

*How to Make Money Marketing Seminars, Workshops and Training Courses*, Bernadette Doyle, 2006

*Info Guru Marketing*, Robert Middleton 2003

*The Life Coach Marketing Bible*, Sean McPheat

# About the author

Jackie Jarvis is an authentic marketing consultant who regularly applies the techniques and suggestions made in her book to both her own business and those of her many small to medium sized business clients. Before setting up Marketingco, Jackie gained her experience across a range of different industries including the media, property, training and coaching, printing, catering, retail and IT.

Through Marketingco she now aims to help SME business owners to 'Make their Marketing Work'.

Marketingco combine expert facilitation with design, copy writing and delivery to enable their customers to get the right message to their right market. Brand image, marketing collateral, advertising and promotional campaigns can all be produced from initial concept through to completed design and print.

Jackie works personally with businesses and their teams on a regular basis facilitating the successful application of all the techniques described in this book. The ongoing relationship providing the expertise, focus and structure required to make sure results are achieved.

Based in Oxfordshire she regularly runs a series of workshops entitled '8 Steps to a Profit Making Marketing Plan' which are designed to facilitate and stimulate the production of that all important marketing plan and the motivation to action it.

The same programme is also available via tele-presentation over eight consecutive weeks.

If you would like a regular injection of 'Marketing Inspiration' and to keep up to date with new products and programmes you can register for a *free* monthly newsletter.

For further details visit *www.marketingco.biz* and for more free reports and marketing resources visit *www.moneymakingmarketingideas.com*

Marketing works...if you work at it...Good luck

Jackie Jarvis

# Preface

## My reason for writing this book

I have written this book for every small business owner and independent professional who wants to make a success of their business marketing. My aim has been to provide you with an easy to read guide full of ideas that ignite your passion for promoting your business and attracting more customers.

During the course of my work with small businesses I found many people frustrated with their marketing effort. Many find it hard work, confusing, time consuming and difficult to get a good return on any investment made. I wrote this book to inspire everyone who feels like this. I want to show you how easy it can be for you to turn things around and start getting the results you deserve.

The ideas presented in this book are practical, real, straightforward and easy for you to apply yourself. This book is designed to be your own pocket marketing consultant. It is there to help you when you need a quick injection of inspiration and when you want to plan your marketing strategy. This book can be all you need to make your marketing work.

## How to use this book step by step

This book is structured in a way to enable you to think about the ideas presented and then apply them to your own business. Starting at the beginning with some of the vital thinking you need to do before embarking on the creation of your marketing plan, you will be guided step by step through the maze. The chapters all logically fit together like the pieces of a jigsaw. Each piece is necessary to create the complete picture.

Reading this book will enable you to create a marketing plan that is exactly right for you.

## Create your marketing plan as you go

With the structure and elements of a marketing plan explained at the start you will be able to move through the chapters one by one, making notes as you go. You can complete your plan section by section. It's as easy as that.

## Pick it up and put it down

This book is also designed to enable you to pick up for a quick idea or an instant reference as you need it. I hope that it will sit on your desk and be referred to from time to time as you need a reminder of the 'How to' guidance or check list information.

## Special response questions

Nearly every section has a check list that contains a number of special response questions. These questions are designed to stimulate the thinking you need to do to be able to apply the ideas presented to you and your business.

## An easy read

I know how busy most small business owners are and that finding the time or motivation to pick up a book can be a struggle. It has been written for you to enjoy with an easy structure to follow, jargon free language, stimulating quotes with questions and ideas that will transform your business marketing.

I do hope that you enjoy this book and it helps you to make your business marketing make you money!

*Jackie Jarvis*

# Introduction

**inspiring ways
to market
your small business**

# 1 Where you are now to where you want to be

Maybe you are wondering if there is a secret to making your marketing work...if there is a special system...a key to success...

Imagine if I told you that the answers you are looking for are inside your own mind and all you really need is the right system, the right questions and the right guidance to enable you to unlock them.

As a successful marketing consultant and business coach I have been amazed by the people I have worked with over the years and how much they have found they already know when stimulated by the right set of questions.

I have written this book to enable more people than I can personally see to benefit from the value of a great marketing idea, the right questions to ask themselves and the prompt for the first vital step they need to take.

## Think your way through the maze

This simple process begins with where you are right now with your business, product or service and takes you to exactly where you want to be. Every step you take will add a vital piece to your ultimate marketing plan of action. At the end of the process you will have a marketing plan that you have created yourself. You will know which marketing strategies are going to offer your particular business the greatest leverage and you will know exactly what you need to do to apply them.

If you need to revive the enthusiasm for your business and bring back the passion you had for it – reading and working through this book is the stimulant you need right now.

If you own a business and you find that you are often too busy 'working *in* the business' to spend time 'working *on* the business' reading this book will inspire you to take time out and move things forward.

Most of all I hope that reading this will provide you with new inspiration and stimulate a new active approach to the successful marketing of your business.

> *Let this book work its magic right now as you turn the page...and stimulate ideas into action...*

# 2 What do you want?

When was the last time you stopped and took a deep breath and asked yourself this question? It is an important one to ask. Under pressure it can be easier to start explaining what you don't want. All that does is reinforce the negative. In order to be able to move forward you need the stimulation of a vision, a goal, and a glimpse of how you would really like things to be. It is a bit like thinking about your holiday plans before you get on the plane. It makes you feel good, motivated, excited. Much better than a good old moan about how you don't want this and you don't want that. Have you ever noticed how that can prompt feelings of the exact opposite to the ones that would help you to move forward and actually get what you do want?

So our very first '**Special Response Question**' is the most important one:

**WHAT IS IT THAT YOU WANT?**
Describe this in all its glory: your business, your work, your lifestyle, your relationships, the way you live your business life, the money you are earning, how you are spending it, what you are doing with your spare time – really let yourself dream.

Write it down and date it.

▶ Where do you want to be 12 months from now?
▶ Where do you want to be three years from now?
▶ What about five years?

Now imagine yourself five years on, having achieved what you want and looking back on yourself today; ask yourself this important question:

▶ What were the most important things you did that enabled you to get where you wanted to be?

Did these questions make you 'think'? Notice how easy it is to shift your mind to a better place when you ask yourself the right question. You may be working hard in your business right now and haven't had time to really 'think' about how you could be growing and developing your business. It might take all your energy just to keep going and get what needs to be done, done.

Questions challenge your thinking, they challenge what you are doing and how you are doing it, they stimulate and most importantly they help you to change things.

# 3 Typical small business marketing mistakes

Making mistakes is part of the learning process. Recognising them is the first important step. Madness has been described as continuing to do the same thing whilst desiring a different result. This is like running an advert week after week in your local publication that never provides a response or reaction and doing nothing about it, whilst at the same time hoping to get a result. There are many examples like this and we are probably all guilty of some of them.

Use the following set of indicators to raise your own awareness of the mistakes you may be making.

- No plan – haphazard activities
- Jumping from one failed idea to another without stopping to think
- Your marketing plan on a 'post it' note or in your head
- Untargeted attempts to generate sales
- Not really knowing what works and what doesn't to make informed decisions
- Trying to do too much too quickly and making mistakes
- Wasting money, time and effort repeating what doesn't work
- Poor decisions about what to invest in – believing the sales person
- No time to do it – suffering from feast and famine revenue cycles
- Mixed messages with no coherent theme
- Too busy *doing* business to consider how to *develop* business
- Over complicating marketing activities and messages
- Believing that you don't have any marketing skills
- Struggling with the 'blank paper' syndrome
- Thinking that marketing is complicated – and avoiding doing it
- Relying on only one or two methods of generating business
- Not keeping good record of your customers' contact details
- Not really being able to explain why someone should buy from you
- Hoping and praying that business will come to you
- Out-dated or weak brand identity

If you have mentally ticked 'yes' that is me in any of the above you are being honest with yourself. We have all been there. You learn by first getting some awareness of what is not working. It is only then that you can start to move forward.

This book will provide you with many of the answers that you have been looking for, as well as help you to action the inspiration it gives you.

# 4 Creating your marketing plan

## What is a marketing plan?

A marketing plan is your guide to exactly how you are going to action your business marketing. It is the ultimate outcome of your thinking and decision making. It is your commitment on paper, your route to success.

## Why is it important?

It is common practice among many small business owners to spend a lot of time *doing* as opposed to planning. You may have a plan in your head that you have not yet committed to paper. Getting out there and making things happen is vital to the success of any small business marketing; it is important, however, that they are the right things. You can spend a lot of time and waste a lot of energy doing things the wrong way or simply just doing the wrong things. A simple marketing plan that you can create yourself using the ideas in this book will keep your business marketing on the right track.

## Your challenge

Your challenge is to take the following eight step plan with their accompanying think marketing questions and create the notes for your plan as you go through the relevant chapters of this book. When you have finished the book you should be in a position to devise a complete marketing strategy that is right for your business.

HERE ARE YOUR EIGHT STEPS TO A SUCCESSFUL PLAN
Each step contains a set of questions that you will need to be able to answer to complete your plan. Reading this book will help you find the answers.

### Step 1 – Understanding your market and your competition
*Your marketplace*
- What is the marketplace within which you are operating?
- What is happening within that marketplace?
- How is the market moving?
- What are the trends?
- What are the hot issues?
- What is the industry press saying?

*Your competition*
- Who do you consider a competitor?
- What are they selling?
- How do they position themselves?
- What is their unique selling proposition?
- What is their competitive edge?
- How much do they charge?
- What marketing literature do they use – what is it like?
- Where are their weaknesses?
- What is their website like?
- What are they not offering that you could?

## Step 2– Understanding your customer

*Your target customer*
- Who is your target customer?
- What are some of the problems your target customer has?
- What is really hot on their agenda right now?
- What is being talked about a lot in the industry press?
- Where is there a 'gap' in the market you are in?
- What would you most like to find out from your target customer?
- What questions could you ask them to enable you to uncover their problems and desires?

*Potential buyers*
- How are potential buyers currently buying what you are selling?
- What are their buying criteria?
- Where do they go to find out what is available?
- When do they tend to buy?
- What do they tend to respond to?
- What problems do they have?
- What solutions are they looking for?

## Step 3 – Positioning your business
- What are your strengths and skills?
- Describe your best and most enjoyable customers to work with.
- What are your broad areas of business and expertise?
- What do you know about the lives and challenges of your customers?
- Describe a number of potential niche customer groups.
- What are these niche groups' problems?
- What could you sell them that would solve their problems?

▶ How are you positioning this business?
▶ What are you selling?

## Step 4 – Developing your marketing message

▶ What is your brand?
▶ What is your USP?
▶ What is your strap-line?
▶ What are your marketing slogans?

## Step 6 – Setting your direction and your marketing goals

▶ What is your vision for your business?
▶ What do you want to achieve with your marketing?
▶ What are your specific and measurable goals for each type of marketing you plan to do?
▶ Can you make each goal SMART – Specific, Measurable, Achievable, Relevant and Time bound?
▶ What are the priorities?
▶ What are your timescales for the achievement of your goals?

## Step 6 – Determining your marketing methods

▶ What marketing methods do you know that your successful competitors use?
▶ What has worked for you in the past? What has been your return on investment (ROI)?
▶ What has not worked?
▶ What can you do to raise your profile in the marketplace?
▶ Which methods can you use to attract new customers?
▶ What potential value do the following marketing methods have for your business? PR, radio, TV, vehicle, bus, posters, billboards, newspapers and magazines advertising, internet, direct mail, sales letters, direct sales, telephone marketing, window displays, personal contact, referrals, host relationships and joint ventures
▶ What is most likely to work best for you?

## Step 7 – Developing your budget

▶ Which marketing methods have you chosen to implement?
▶ What is it going to cost to utilise your chosen marketing methods?
▶ What resources are going to be required to implement these methods?
▶ What will you need to invest in each segment to achieve your goals?
▶ What return would you expect?
▶ How will you measure the return on your investment?

### Step 8 – Planning your strategy

▶ How are you going to progress each element of your plan?

▶ What needs setting up?

▶ What are the priorities?

▶ What specific practical actions need to be taken to make it happen? By whom and by when?

▶ What are the steps?

▶ What are the milestones and deadlines?

▶ How will you monitor, evaluate and review your strategy?

## *Create your marketing plan*

Here are the headings for the important sections of your marketing plan: You can use this template as a framework for your own plan, which can be completed as you work through the sections in this book.*

**Business description** – who are you and what do you do

**Market** – your industry, broad area of business operation

**Competition** – who they are, what they offer, strengths and weaknesses

**Target customer group(s)** – who you are aiming at

**Target market area(s)** – the area(s) you want your business to come from

**Niche description** – your target specialist area and business positioning

**Marketing message** – your brand, strap-line, USP and slogans

**Marketing goals and objectives** – what you want to achieve

**Marketing methods** – the methods you have chosen to utilise

**The budget** – the amount you commit to spending

**The strategy** – how you are going to do this and calendar of actions

> ***Fail to plan – plan to fail***

*If you would like a *free* electronic version of this Marketing Plan template you can download one from www.moneymakingmarketingideas.com

# 2

# How to get started – evaluating where you are now

**inspiring ways
to market
your small business**

# 5 Defining your business now

## *The journey begins from where you are now...*

You are where you are now as a direct result of the actions you have taken and the decisions you have made along the way. Where you will get to in the future will be a result of the choices you make, starting now. Imagine today as the first day of the rest of your business life.

## *Why take stock first?*

It is important to assess exactly where you are now before you embark on your journey. Many people are so busy *doing* that they rarely take the time out to take stock and reflect. It is vital, from time to time, to take that vital step back from the cut and thrust of your daily workload. If you keep on doing what you have always been doing, you will always get what you have now.

## *Your challenge*

You will need to be honest with yourself and focus on the facts. This may involve some detail that you haven't paid attention to for a while. You will need to be disciplined as you gather this information. Don't rely on guess work or gut feel. Get the specifics as it is these details that will form the bedrock from which you can move forward. If you want to grow your business you will need to know exactly where you are starting from.

---

YOUR BUSINESS NOW – SPECIAL RESPONSE CHECKLIST

*Your business*
- ▶ Describe your business right now. What words express exactly where you feel you are? Brainstorm and just jot down what comes to mind.
- ▶ Make a list of the main services/products that you offer.
- ▶ What is selling well?
- ▶ What isn't selling well?

*Turnover and profit margins*
- ▶ What is your turnover?
- ▶ What is your current end of year profit?

*Customers*
- ▶ How many customers do you have?
- ▶ Where do they come from?
- ▶ What kind of profile do they have?
- ▶ Who are your best customers?
- ▶ Who are your worst customers?

*Business strengths*
- ▶ What are the key strengths your business has?
- ▶ What are the key skills contained within this business?

*Your attitude towards your business*
- ▶ How do you feel about your business?
- ▶ What do you find difficult?
- ▶ What is it that you like and enjoy?

## How to use this information

Having answered these questions you will have some specific facts, thoughts and feelings to work with. You now have a starting point. This is where you are now. It is a good idea to mark the date in your diary or on your calendar when you did this exercise. This information gives you a basis from which to start to think about your future and where you want to go.

# 6 Evaluating how well your current marketing is working

## What is marketing?

Marketing is everything that you do to communicate your business to both your existing and potential customers. There are many different ways that you can market your business. Most people use a combination that works best for their particular business.

## What works and what doesn't?

If you are spending money on marketing your business it is vital that you know what works and what doesn't. There is no point in investing money when what you are doing is not bringing you a good return. So how do you know whether it is working or not?

## Your challenge

Your main challenge is continually to test and measure your marketing efforts. Relying on gut feel is not enough. You will need some tangible feedback. Try the following checklist indicating what you have tried and whether it was successful or not. Note down any tangible evidence that you have to support your definition of success. Have a look at this marketing evaluation checklist and evaluate how successful you consider your marketing efforts, to have been to date.

**CURRENT MARKETING EVALUATION CHECKLIST**
**Which of the following have you tried and how successful has it been?**
**Rate each area: 1 = no success, 5 = very successful**

| | | | | | |
|---|---|---|---|---|---|
| Brand identity | 1 | 2 | 3 | 4 | 5 |
| Newspaper advertising | 1 | 2 | 3 | 4 | 5 |
| Advertorial | 1 | 2 | 3 | 4 | 5 |
| Radio advertising | 1 | 2 | 3 | 4 | 5 |
| TV advertising | 1 | 2 | 3 | 4 | 5 |
| PR/articles | 1 | 2 | 3 | 4 | 5 |
| Direct mail | 1 | 2 | 3 | 4 | 5 |
| Sales letter | 1 | 2 | 3 | 4 | 5 |

| | | | | | |
|---|---|---|---|---|---|
| Networking | 1 | 2 | 3 | 4 | 5 |
| Telemarketing | 1 | 2 | 3 | 4 | 5 |
| Events/talks | 1 | 2 | 3 | 4 | 5 |
| Newsletter | 1 | 2 | 3 | 4 | 5 |
| Website marketing | 1 | 2 | 3 | 4 | 5 |
| Referrals/recommendation | 1 | 2 | 3 | 4 | 5 |
| Sales person | 1 | 2 | 3 | 4 | 5 |
| Window displays | 1 | 2 | 3 | 4 | 5 |
| Host relationships | 1 | 2 | 3 | 4 | 5 |
| Special offers | 1 | 2 | 3 | 4 | 5 |
| Email marketing | 1 | 2 | 3 | 4 | 5 |

## *How successfully to test and measure your marketing*

You can do this in a number of ways.

- Ask the people who enquire where they heard about your business.

- Keep a note of this information over a defined period of time and analyse it.

- Run specific offers in selected marketing options and keep a record of responses.

- Test headlines on adverts or flyers in smaller batches until you find out which gets the best result.

- You can do the same with sales letters sent by post and email.

- When you run an event, or speak at a networking group, keep a record of how many contacts you make and whether any business results from them.

- Do the same for networking events you attend as a participant.

- When you write an article for a business publication offer a free report that requires the reader to make contact with you. This way you will not only get the details of some potentially good prospects but you can test how many people read and responded to your article.

- Before and after sales data is useful when you are running a brand awareness campaign.

### MARKETING EVALUATION – SPECIAL RESPONSE CHECKLIST
▶ Decide how you are going to evaluate your activities in advance.
▶ Keep a record of the evaluation data you collect.

▶ Work out which has been the most successful marketing activity.

▶ Plan to repeat all successful activities.

▶ Ask yourself why certain activities have not been successful.

▶ Check that the marketing activities you have chosen are right for the audience you wish to target.

▶ Stop any expensive marketing activity that is costing more than the return it gives you.

## *How to use this information*

Over a period of time, monitoring and measuring the success of your marketing will enable you to build a very clear picture of how to spend your valuable marketing budget. There will be no more last minute decisions or trial and error, as you will have the evidence you need at your fingertips, and you will be able to use the information to make informed decisions.

> *Think, test and measure*

# 7 Assessing the value of your current base

## Growing your current customer base

There are three main ways to grow any business:

- get new customers
- increase the amount your existing customers spend with you
- increase the frequency with which they do business with you.

It is easier and less expensive to build on the existing base you already have than it is to develop new customer relationships.

## What is the value of your current customer base?

Do you know?

To work out the average value of your current customer base all you need to do is find the following figures.

- How many customers do you have?
- What is the average amount these customers spend with you?
- How many times a year do these customers spend this amount?
- What is the average length of time your customers stay doing business with you?

$$\text{Number} \, x \, \text{value} \, x \, \text{frequency} = \text{value of current customer}$$
$$\text{base} \, x \, \text{length of time as a customer}$$
$$100 \times £1{,}000 \times 3 = £300{,}000 \times 2 \text{ years} = £600{,}000$$

Based on these figures each new customer you get is potentially worth £6,000.

## Why is this important?

It is important to know what your current customer base is potentially worth to you, as it gives you a starting point, a base from which to decide how you want to grow your business.

If you use the marketing techniques detailed in this book to

■ attract new customers
■ get existing customers to spend more
■ get existing customers to spend more often

you could potentially increase your profits by whatever figure you decide you want. There is a vast amount of untapped potential in your business right now. All you need to do is decide what you want and then get really good at marketing to make it happen.

Your existing customer base probably holds the most potential for you. These are people who are already happily doing business with you. They already spend money regularly and probably would spend more if they had a good reason to. You need to give them that reason.

## Your challenge

Your challenge is to both maintain and develop the value of your existing customer base. No business can afford to stand still.

## What makes a customer base valuable?

If you can answer yes to the following questions, your existing customer base has value.

■ Do your existing customers spend money with you?
■ Are they happy with the service you provide?
■ Have you built up a relationship of trust and rapport?
■ Do they come to you for the solutions to their problems?
■ If asked, would they recommend or refer you to other people?
■ Are they likely to have needs in the future and problems they want solving?
■ Would they spend more with you if you could help them?

CUSTOMER VALUE – SPECIAL RESPONSE CHECKLIST
Get specific with your customer sales information.

▶ Create a list of your main customers.

- ► How many customers do you have?
- ► Where do they come from?
- ► How much does each customer spend with you every year?
- ► How often does each customers use you?
- ► What are their particular spending patterns?
- ► What interests does each customer have in your business?
- ► What potential does each customer have to spend more with you?

## *How to use this information*

Once you know the value of your existing client base you have a starting place. Once you have specific customer information you can work out which business building strategy will be most likely to appeal to particular customer groups or individuals. If you think of each new customer having a life time value potential it makes it even more important to value them right from the start, no matter how little they start off spending with you.

> **Think customer = pot of gold**

# 8 Finding out what existing customers value about your business

## What is customer feedback?

Customer feedback is the information that you get from your customers about the work that you do for them, positive and negative. How do you get yours? There are several different ways in which feedback can be gathered.

- Best and worst selling products/services.
- Repeat business.
- Behaviour and body language observation.
- Questions asked.
- Complaints.
- Verbal comments.
- Conversations with customers.
- Testimonials and letters.
- Recommendations.
- Survey information.

## Why is this important?

It is important to be aware of the feedback you are getting from your customers. This is how you learn about what is and isn't important to the people you wish to influence. If you are selling something that people want and you are delivering value, you need to know about it!

This is information that you can use to attract more customers. It is also a confidence boost for you if you know how much people value what you offer. You can allow yourself to feel good and very proud of what you are doing. If your business is missing what customers value most, you need to know about that as well. This information can teach you how to make your business more attractive to the people that you value most: your customers.

## Your challenge

Your challenge is to set up a system both to gather and evaluate this information on a regular basis. You need to be open and able to listen to customers' views. You will need to be prepared to ask and develop questions that are targeted to extract the right information. When asking for customer feedback you will need to be careful about guiding the customer's mind in the right direction. If you ask 'What didn't you like about the service today?' the response can only be negative. Whereas if you say 'What did you think about the service today?' and give a choice of responses, there is a greater chance of a positive result.

**WHAT DO YOU NEED TO KNOW – SPECIAL RESPONSE CHECKLIST**

- What are people buying?
- What do people want to buy?
- What are their service expectations?
- What is really important in terms of product/service delivery?
- What irritates and frustrates people?

*Great questions to ask*

- When choosing a [your service] what do you look for?
- When buying [your service] what is most important?
- What prompted the decision to use x services?
- What have you found of most value?
- What (if anything) could we do to improve the x service we offer you?
- What do you like about x ?
- Which aspect of x do you find of most value?

Depending on whether you are using a written or telephone survey, or holding a one-to-one conversation the way you organise your questions will vary. You may use multichoice, with a range from most important to least important, or leave them open for comments. The important thing is that you make it easy for people to answer the questions when you ask them. Any surveys you do ideally should comprise no more than 10 questions. If you are conducting a telephone survey and you get some really positive statements always ask if you can quote them. This is a very easy and quick way of getting testimonials.

## How to use this information

A list of what your customers most value about your business can be used to help you create all your marketing messages, your brand, your unique selling proposition, your customer commitment statement, your list of attractive benefits, your website or brochure copy and even your elevator speech. Knowing what customers value is invaluable to you.

> **Think feedback and learn more**

# 9 Seeing your business through the customers' eyes

## What does this mean?

If you want to influence your customers you have to understand and relate to them. When you see through your customers' eyes you experience the world from a different perspective. Imagine you have taken your customers' glasses and you are looking at your business through those lenses. What do you see? Do you suddenly see it all differently? You should. Many business owners find this exercise extremely difficult to do. Be careful that you don't get so close to your own business by running it day-to-day that you stop being able to see things from your customers' point of view.

## Why this is important

It is important to switch perspectives from time to time. Making decisions about shop layout, website design, customer communication processes and more becomes a lot easier when you are able to imagine yourself as the customer. You will avoid the classic pitfalls that many people make when they make elements of their service over complicated and confusing. Most people these days want things simply, quickly and easily. If it is complicated, slow or difficult your potential customers will go somewhere else. This is especially true of the internet age which has brought with it choice and speed. Very few have the patience to wait.

## Your challenge

Your challenge will be to spend the time taking a look at your business through your customers' eyes and maintain this perspective for long enough to gain some valuable insights.

**WHAT DO YOU NEED TO DO? – SPECIAL RESPONSE CHECKLIST**
- ▶ Take some time out and close your eyes.
- ▶ Think about one of your typical customers.
- ▶ Describe that person to yourself.
   What are they like?
   How old are they?
   What typically do they do each day?

What is important to them?

What are they looking for when they consider buying *x*?

▶ Now imagine yourself as this person coming along to your business or finding you on the internet.

What do you see?

What is your first impression?

What do you feel?

▶ Check out every individual aspect of your business from this perspective. You can enter your website as a customer, you can use your service as a customer, you can pretend to have a complaint as a customer. You can look at your advertising – any number of things. Look at what goes on in your business through your customers' eyes.

▶ Note down the things that you see.

▶ Try seeing through the eyes of a number of different types of customers.

▶ Notice what is different and what is similar.

## How to use this information

You can use this information to make changes to your business operations and your marketing. If you do, make sure that you monitor the results of those changes. Notice the impact that they have on your customers. Take time out to switch perspectives as often as you can. It is a skill that you can develop and one that is very useful to your business. Many top business entrepreneurs are very good at this. Think about Richard Branson for example. He regularly takes time out to see his businesses through his customers' eyes.

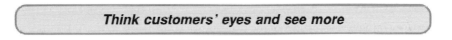

**Think customers' eyes and see more**

# 10 Assessing your personal strengths, skills and resources

## What are your strengths, skills and resources?

There is no doubt that your own personal strengths, skills and resources are a major reason for your achievements to date. They are sure to play a major part in the success of your business. They may well be the main reason that your customers choose to use your service or buy your products. Are you aware of exactly what those strengths, skills and resources actually are? You can take them for granted because they are with you every day. Being too close to yourself can make you blind to your own brilliance.

## Why is it important to know?

Your strengths and skills are unique to you and could be a major part of what differentiates you from others in the marketplace. They are also a major reason for the value placed on any advice and consultancy you may give your customers.

Your strengths and skills are part of your history, the history that created the business you have today. You may have spent years developing these skills. You may have years and years of experience behind you. Your customers may not necessarily know anything about this. If they did, the question is, would they see more value in what you offer?

An awareness of and the ability to communicate the strengths and skills you have is a very important part of your business marketing. You are at the centre of what you are selling and the more value you place on that, the more others are likely to as well. It can help you to communicate what you do more effectively to the prospects and new contacts you meet. This may form part of the process you go through to help them to appreciate the true value you are able to offer.

## Your challenge

Your challenge will be to become self aware and find a useful way of making your customers aware too. Your challenge may also be to see the value in yourself and what you have to offer. Many of us are conditioned not to blow our own trumpet and to be modest about those things we are good at. That is fine, but you must not ignore the things that your customers would value and have a right to know about.

Your customers and prospects want the best. They want someone whom they can trust to provide top quality expertise and deliver with skill. If that person is you, then you are duty bound to tell them.

**SELF AWARENESS – SPECIAL RESPONSE CHECKLIST**
▶ What do you think your main strengths are?
▶ How do these strengths impact on your business?
▶ What are your key skills?
▶ How have you developed these skills?
▶ What kinds of experiences have enabled you to gain this expertise?
▶ How essential are these skills to the service you are able to offer your customers?
▶ Which of your skills is valued most by your customers?
▶ What parts of your personal history have had an impact on the strengths and skills you are now able to demonstrate?
▶ What kind of training and education have you had?
▶ What resources do you have access to as a result of your experiences?
▶ What is your special story?

## *How to use this information*

Going through the special response questions may make you see the true value you bring to the table. Once your eyes are opened to your own brilliance you may find yourself feeling more confident and more self assured. It is empowering to feel that as a result of all your hard work and effort developing skills, strengths and resources that you are really worth something. The benefit **you** offer your business can be integrated into your marketing messages and materials. There will be plenty of opportunity to find exactly how to do this as you read later chapters of this book.

> *Think personal strength and sell 'you'*

# Getting clear about where you are going

**inspiring ways
to market
your small business**

# 11 Clarifying your ultimate business vision

## What is a vision?

A vision is the picture or movie you see in your mind's eye of the future. It is the dream you have of the reality you want to be living. Your vision can be imagined by using your senses to see, feel and hear a 'what if' experience. It is a bit like the experience you have when you imagine your perfect holiday destination. You have a 'vision' of the kind of holiday you would most like to experience.

## Why is it important?

Creating a vision is a way of anticipating the future. It is like planting a seed in your mind which, if you feed and water correctly, over time will grow and flower in the way that it was predestined to.

By allowing yourself to project into the future in this way you can check out if you like what you see. Describing your vision can inspire both you and the others in your team. Everyone needs something to aim for. It is like describing the view you will have at the mountain top before you start the climb. The motivation you have for the potentially arduous journey will be boosted more by being very clear about what you will see at the top than it would have been if it had been just a climb. It can be exactly the same with your business. If you have a clear and exciting vision in your mind, a vision that you can communicate to others, the journey will be much more energised and focused. Having a vision makes day-to-day activities more meaningful as you have a reason for doing them.

## Your challenge

Your vision not only needs to be something that you aspire to business wise, but also something that fits in with your personal life goals. The two go hand in hand. It is no good having a vision for a business future that would involve work overseas and long periods of time away from home if one of your personal goals is to spend more time with your family. It is important to clarify your personal goals and incorporate them into your vision for the future.

## What makes a vision reality?

To make your vision a reality you will need to take action today. Your daily choices of action will ultimately make the difference between getting there or staying put. Having a vision alone is not enough to make it happen.

**SEEING YOUR VISION – SPECIAL RESPONSE QUESTIONS**

Take a few moments to relax and take a walk into the future. Close your eyes and imagine yourself in this place where everything you wanted has been achieved.

▶ What do you see happening in your business?
▶ What does it look like?
▶ What kind of clients do you see?
▶ Who else do you see working with you?
▶ What are you doing?
▶ What are people saying about your business?
▶ What are you saying?
▶ What are you feeling?
▶ What are others feeling about the business you have created?

*Looking back*

From this place having achieved everything you wanted, imagine yourself turning back and seeing yourself as you are now. Ask:

▶ What were some of the most important things you did to get here?
▶ What is the best advice you can give yourself?

*Taking it with you*

Now imagine yourself taking this advice with you as you start your journey towards your vision.

*Writing it down*

Having done this exercise it is a good idea to write a description of your business vision. That way you can remind yourself of it from time to time, add to it or adapt as things change. Find a visual image that you relate to. Pin it up on the wall where you can see it every day. This will keep you anchored to your future.

## How to use your vision

Once you have a vision, you can use it to motivate both yourself and others. Describing the ultimate vision can be the first step needed to kick start a strategic planning meeting with your team. Your business goals and objectives should come out of the vision and your strategic action plan will be guided by your business goals and objectives. Your marketing strategy will be part of your overall business plan guided by your business vision. Marketing your business successfully will be one of the important actions you need to take to get you to your ultimate destination.

> **Think vision and see your future success in advance**

## 12 Defining the gaps between present and desired

### What is a defined gap?

So far in this book you have had a chance to think about where you are now with your business and where you want to be in the future. Unless you are living your vision right now there will be a gap between these two points – present and desired. You need to be clear about exactly what is missing. Creating a defined gap is about getting very specific about the elements of your business that you need to focus on in order to close the gap and achieve your ultimate goals. The gap between present and desired position will differ from business to business.

Here are some examples of the general gaps you might find yourself defining.

- Personal activities (time and focus).
- Quality of products and services.
- Location.
- Number of outlets.
- Market area.
- Target customers.
- Numbers of customers.
- Systems and procedures.
- Marketing activities.
- Staff team.
- Knowledge.
- Skills.

### Why is it important to define the gaps?

Defining the gaps specifically is important because it will focus your attention on what needs work. Once you have clearly defined the gaps then they can be used to set appropriate goals and objectives with a plan to achieve them. Without defining the gaps it could be very easy to slip into the grass-hopper approach to business and marketing planning, jumping from one thing to the next or allowing yourself to get distracted.

## Your challenge

Your challenge is to take the time to do this. To focus on what needs your attention. Be honest with yourself. This will pay dividends in the longer term.

At this stage you do not have to have the solution. That comes later. All you need to do is be very clear about what needs your attention. It may be that you don't know what needs work or needs to be implemented to get you from where you are to where you want to be. If that is the case you could come back to this chapter once you have got to the end of this book. It would be useful to keep a notebook to hand and write down gaps as you come across them.

### GETTING TO THE GAP – SPECIAL RESPONSE CHECKLIST
▶ In front of you have your notes from 'where you are now' along with your ultimate business vision.
▶ Make a note of some of the problems you perceive you have now that may prevent you from reaching your vision. These problem areas will indicate gaps.
▶ Make a note of all the areas of your business where you see a clear gap.
▶ For each of those areas write down what the gap is.

## How to use this information

This information can be used in a number of ways. Firstly the gaps you establish will highlight the information you need to gather, the processes you need to implement, the changes you need to make and the goals you need to set. Secondly it will give your thinking some structure, and focus your attention on the important issues to consider when business planning. Thirdly they will remind you of what is vital if you are to achieve your vision. Talking about it is not enough to make it happen – it needs action focused in the most important areas.

> **Think gap and make the right things happen**

# 13 Describing who you want to do business with

## Defining your ideal customer

Defining your ideal customer means clarifying the people who are, or are likely to be, hungry for your particular product or service. Your ideal customers will be people who have a problem that they are searching for an answer to. They will be people who are most likely to spend money on your product or service to fulfil a need or desire they have. Your ideal target customer could have certain demographic, psychographic, occupational or geographic characteristics.

## Why is this important?

Knowing who it is you are targeting will greatly influence how you go about communicating your product or service to them. Ideally if you can find a hungry crowd for your particular niche product or service and can understand very clearly what their particular needs and problems are, you can tailor your marketing messages to fulfil those needs and solve those problems. This will mean your marketing can be targeted. Ideally for the greatest chance of success, your business will initially have been created to fill a need or solve the problems of a particular customer group.

## Your challenge

Your challenge will be in how you go about finding your ideal customer. If you are an existing and established business you will have details of your existing customers and knowledge of what and how much they have bought from you over time. There may be certain patterns; things that your existing customer groups have in common that you could learn from. Your challenge will be in taking the time to analyse the data that you have right on your own doorstep. You can also learn from the customers that you don't have yet, the ones that you think might be ideal for your business. These are the people who you need to find out about, what their problems are, what they want and what they are willing to spend money on. This will involve some targeted research.

## *What makes a customer ideal?*

- They want what you are selling.
- They are willing and able to pay for it.
- There are a lot of them.
- You know how to get access them.
- You like working with them.
- You find them easy to sell your product or service to.
- They are most likely to keep on buying from you.

### IDEAL CUSTOMER – SPECIAL RESPONSE CHECKLIST

To establish your ideal customer you will need to ask yourself some questions.

▶ Describe the kind of person who could be most hungry for your product or service.
▶ Who have your best customers been in the past?
▶ What have your best customers had in common?
▶ What kinds of people/organisations do you really like working with?
▶ What kind of problems and needs do they have?
▶ Where ideally are these companies/people located?

## *How to use this Information*

First of all you need to test your ideal customer description by asking some questions and doing some research. Once you are sure that this customer fulfils all of your criteria then you will need to design both your marketing message and your marketing materials to influence this customer positively.

> *Think ideal customer and do business with the best*

# Understanding your marketplace and your competition

**inspiring ways
to market
your small business**

# 14 Researching for answers

## What is research?

Research is everything you do to find out about your customer, marketplace and competition that will enable you to build a clear picture of what is most likely to sell well. Research can be surveys, asking questions, listening, the observation of trends, mystery shopper trips, surfing the internet, attending conferences and events, your own experience of life, reading articles or becoming a member of an association.

## Why is it important?

The more you know about your potential client, competitors and your potential marketplace the better placed you will be to make decisions about the best positioning and packaging of your products and services. Research can help you to find out what your ideal target customer is most likely to buy. It can enable you to package your products and services to fit with demand rather than the other way round. Research can help save you time and money. You can get answers from research that could have taken years of trial and error to find out.

## What makes research work?

It works when it is pre-planned and when you have a clear outcome in mind. You need to be very clear on the reasons for the research and what specifically you are looking for.

You should choose the research method that best suits the outcome you want. You may run a survey online that enables you to question large numbers of people and provides full analysis in report format, or you may think asking questions one to one is a better way to get the answers you need from a smaller test selection of people. Whichever way you choose, you will need to compare like for like. Ask people the same questions and compare answers. Look for both similarities and differences. Look for patterns and trends. Deciding on a way of recording and analysing the data is important. A simple self created spreadsheet may well be enough to record some basic research data.

**Examples**

A show jumping club wanted to raise its membership prices in addition to attracting new members from a wider section of the show jumping community. Its reason for running a research survey was to find out what people wanted from the club and potentially what was most important in terms of club events, trips and hospitality. This information would help them to design the members' package to suit members' desires. They also wanted to gain buy-in to price changes by offering greater value. They used a pre-designed ten question survey which they sent out to both existing members and a cross-section of people they would like as members.

A garage planning the expansion of their services in the local area needed to find out who else offered the services they had in mind and at what price. They also needed to find out if their existing customer base had a need or desire for these additional services, and would use them if offered. This information would help them to decide whether or not it was a good idea to introduce the services. They used telephone research with existing customers and mystery shopper visits to the competition.

## *Learning from the competition*

Take the time to find out. Call up some of your competitors posing as a customer and ask some questions. Find out what they are doing, what they are offering, what their sales process is and their prices. Listen to how they are presenting their service. Look at their websites.

## *Learning from your customers (existing and potential)*

The people who use your product or service are the best people to give you feedback. Ask questions when you get the chance. Listen to the responses. Ask for specific information as opposed to general comments. Pay attention to the questions you get asked. Often this is an indication of what they need. Observe the decision making process of your customers. How long do they take? Understand what is either motivating or preventing them from buying.

### CUSTOMER RESEARCH – SPECIAL RESPONSE CHECKLIST

▶ Discuss what it is that you need to find out and write it down.

▶ Create some questions that make it easy for customers to answer with specifics (multi-choice, most or least important, order of importance are helpful when creating surveys).

▶ Keep the surveys brief – no more than ten questions is best.

▶ If you are asking questions verbally no more than five questions is best.

▶ Decide how you are going to record the information to be able to compare like with like.

▶ Pay attention to your results and adapt as necessary.

## How to use this information

This information is invaluable for use creating the positioning and packaging of your products and services. It is essential for developing your unique selling proposition which is covered later on in this book. Marketing messages that target customers' desires and motivations can be created with minimum fuss and wastage. With information about the customer you are able to speak their language.

> **Think research and learn**

# 15 Evaluating your competitors' propositions

Evaluating your competitors' propositions is all about studying exactly how they are positioning and presenting themselves. It is about exploring what they are doing and seeing for yourself where their strengths and weaknesses are.

## Why is it important?

This is important because your competitors are in your marketplace and you will no doubt come up against their propositions when you take your service to market. It is useful to understand exactly what they are offering to see whether there is anything you could learn about and/or do better or differently.

## Your challenge

Your challenge will be to find out. It takes time to study your competitors and it needs to be done in a systematic way to get the best out of the exercise.

## How to check out your competition

You can be a real customer. You can visit their premises and read their advertising and promotional literature. You can visit their websites. You can subscribe to their newsletters. You can call in as a mystery shopper.

EVALUATING YOUR COMPETITION – SPECIAL RESPONSE CHECKLIST

These are the questions you need answers to:

▶ Who do you consider a competitor?
▶ What are they selling?
▶ How do they position themselves?
▶ What is their unique selling proposition?
▶ What is their competitive edge?
▶ How much do they charge?
▶ What marketing literature do they use – what is it like?
▶ Where are the weaknesses?
▶ What is their website like?
▶ What are they not offering that you could?

▶ What questions would you like to ask as a potential customer?

▶ Would you use this product or service?

## How to use this information

A useful way to summarise this information and compare notes at a glance is to create a spreadsheet and compare like with like.*

> **Think evaluate the competition and get the edge**

*download your free competitor evaluation spreadsheet from *www.marketingco.biz* (templates section) or from www.moneymakingmarketingideas.com

# 16 Learning from others in your marketplace

All successful business owners have been through a learning curve to enable them to get to where they are now. You may be just about to start that journey. There are many sources of learning for you if you know where to look and are prepared to go out there and ask for the information you need.

## Who can you learn from?

Depending on what you want to know the sources are endless.

### Role models

Find a number of potential role models, people who are currently doing exactly what you want to do and doing it well. When I wanted to get a book publishing opportunity I asked a number of published authors about their experiences and how they went about getting a book deal. I am now doing the same for other information products that I wish to produce. Model the best.

### Real-life experiences

Read books about the 'real story' behind businesses that have achieved phenomenal success in the marketplace. Most you will find started from humble beginnings. Read about Sahar and Bobby Hashemi in their book *Anyone Can Do It – Building Coffee Republic From Our Kitchen Table*, Richard Branson and Virgin and Anita Roddick and The Body Shop.

### Entrepreneurs

Do you know any entrepreneurs? They make their ideas happen. Most entrepreneurs you will find have had a number of failed experiences before their big break took place.

### Marketers and specialists

What about successful marketers who will also have plenty to share? These are specialists in the particular areas of expertise that you know you need to make your business a success.

*Other business owners*

Somewhere in the country there will be other businesses just like yours which are successful. They may be willing to share their secrets with you as long as they see that you are not a competitor. Many people like to help.

*The media*

There are marketing ideas around you everywhere you go. Notice what has an impact on you. Could you adapt that idea in any way to work for your business?

## What can you learn?

You will need to be clear about what it is that you need to learn before you embark on your quest. Here are some suggestions.

- Systems and methods.
- Problems that you might come up against and how others found a way through.
- Marketing ideas.
- Typical mistakes to avoid.
- Suppliers of services you need to make your business a success.

## Why is learning important?

Why reinvent the wheel? If what you want to do is currently being done successfully somewhere then it can save you enormous amounts of time, energy and resources if you can find out where and learn from the person who did it. It can take a long time to work it out for yourself. There is so much information available and so many ideas that you can benefit from that you don't need to feel alone with the thoughts in your own head and a blank piece of paper.

## Your challenge

Be careful to choose the right sources and people to speak to. Some people may put you off with too many negative experiences. You need to be selective about what you take on board and what you let go.

## What can help you to learn?

To start with accept that it is okay not to know all the answers. An open, inquisitive mind is the best place to start from. It is useful to have a structure to your quest. Know what you want to find out. You also need a plan to do something with the information as you get it. Remember 'what you don't use you lose'.

**LEARNING FROM OTHERS IN YOUR MARKETPLACE – SPECIAL RESPONSE CHECKLIST**
- Write a list of all the things you want to know.
- Write down some questions you want answers to.
- Decide how you are going to find this information.
- Find out who are the best people to speak to.
- Who do you know who could help brainstorm?
- Decide on the best sources of the information you need.
- Make a plan.
- Decide how you are going to keep a record of it.

*Questions for your role models and similar successful and respected businesses*
- Looking back at your success what was the most important thing you did?
- What were the biggest challenges you faced?
- How did you overcome these challenges?
- How did you build a successful marketing system?
- What is most important to set up initially?
- What works best for you?
- Looking back, knowing what you know now, what would you pay most attention to?

## How to use this information

It is important to take what learning you need from your role models and do something with it as soon as you can.

Take other people's ideas and make them your own. Use their experience to stimulate ideas for your own business. Make it a goal to practise life-long learning.

> *Think role model and learn from what already works*

# 5

# Understanding your customer

**inspiring ways
to market
your small business**

# 17 Finding out about your target customer

## What does this mean?

Your target customer is someone who has the need, desire, time and money to do business with you. Finding out about them is about doing whatever you can to get an insight into their lives, habits, likes, dislikes, problems and aspirations. It is all about finding out what they want to buy now and in the future.

## Why is it important?

It is important to find out as much as you can about your potential target customers. This information will help you to sell to them, market and promote your business in the right way for them and ultimately influence them positively. The more you know, the more you can do to ensure you hit the right spot with every step you take towards converting them from prospect to enthusiastic user of your products and services.

Finding out about your target customer will help you to establish the quality of the market for your products and services. You need to know that your product or service is attractive to the people you want to buy it.

The more you know about your target customers, the more targeted your marketing efforts can be. The more targeted they are, the less likely you are to suffer wastage in time, effort and money.

## Your challenge

Being very specific about your target customer can be a hard thing for some business owners to do. Depending on your business type there may be many different targets. Think back to the ideal target customer you described after reading Chapter 3. Are there one or two specific groups of people that you need to know as much as possible about?

If you have been in business for a while it can be easy to make assumptions about the people you do business with and decide what it is that you think they want. This can be a dangerous thing to do. People change, their desires and needs change and new problems are arising all the time. To continue to make a success of the communication of your business to the right people you need to be continually finding out about them.

## What to find out about your target customer

- Their demographic profile: for individuals – gender, age, income, education, occupation, location; for companies – industry type, number of employees, location
- Their psychographics – these are the things that relate to the character of the individuals you do business with
- Their interests and habits
- Their location and how to reach them
- Where they may be currently looking for the solutions like yours
- How they go about buying the products or services you are selling
- How they like to buy
- What they are comfortable paying
- The impact of special offers or packaging
- Where they go to find products or services like yours
- The particular things that are important to them when they are buying a service or product like yours

### YOUR SPECIAL RESPONSE CHECKLIST
- ▶ How much do you already know about your target customers?
- ▶ What can you do to constantly update this information?
- ▶ What are the evolving problems of your target customers?
- ▶ What is happening in the market in general that may be about to influence them?
- ▶ What are the main problems your target customer has that your product or service could fulfil?
- ▶ Describe some of the habits your target customers have.
- ▶ What do they read, where do they go, what are they interested in?
- ▶ What is the best route to your target customer?
- ▶ How could you find out the answers to the questions you have?

## How to find out this information

There are many ways in which you could do this. The first is as simple as asking questions. A networking event is a useful forum for doing this one to one. Another alternative is a focus group. This is where you arrange to get together a small group of people who represent the range of those you see as typical of your target customer. You may need to offer an incentive for these people to help you with your research. You can also run surveys that ask a selection of pertinent questions.

Observation is also a very useful way to see what your target customer responds to, and what is currently available for them. Visiting competitors' business premises as a customer and just watching what goes on can give you a lot of useful information. Sahar Hashemi the successful entrepreneur who founded the Coffee Republic took, as part of her initial customer research, the Circle Line round London, stopping at every junction to see what was available for business people and shoppers who wanted a nice cup of coffee.

Taking the time to talk to the customers who use your business now is a great way to keep up with their changing needs.

The internet, industry press, survey reports and books are all rich sources of information about your target customer.

## How to use this information

Finding out about your target customers is a continual process of exploration and interest. It is useful to develop a system to do this year on year. Don't make decisions behind closed doors and never forget to keep in very close touch with the people that are vital to your business success – your customers.

> *Think about, ask and understand your target customer better*

# 18 Understanding what people buy

## What do people buy?

When people buy goods and services what is it that they are really buying? It is not so much about what the product or service is as about an important outcome getting fulfilled. People buy outcomes. They buy the important result they want at the time. What does someone buy when they get a hair cut? It is not just shorter hair they want, but the ultimate outcome of looking good. What does someone buy when they buy a meal out in a restaurant? It is not just food that they want to eat, but a fun and social interaction with friends or family perhaps. People buy either to satisfy a positive or to avoid a negative outcome. People move towards pleasure or away from pain. Fear of loss can be as big a driving force as pleasure in gain. Here are some examples of outcomes that people buy in a variety of purchasing contexts.

- Results
- Support
- Avoidance of worry
- Escape from pain
- Avoidance of losing money
- Answers
- Improvements
- Enhancements
- Time and effort saving
- Joy
- Self-respect
- Benefits

- Value
- Advantages
- Reliability
- Freedom
- Fulfilment
- Happiness
- Solutions
- Time-saving
- Pleasure
- Prestige
- Reward
- Protection

## What motivates decisions?

Buying decisions are motivated by what is important to a person. What is important is connected with personal values. A value is something that matters deeply to a person. Your values create mental filters which search for satisfaction when choosing a product or service. In order to influence you will need to address the satisfaction of these values in your presentation. Notice how some of the following marketing messages address customers' values.

Sainsbury's – 'Making life taste better'
Home Base – 'Making a house a home'

Norwich Union Direct – 'Let us quote you happy'
Audi – 'In pursuit of perfection'
Printinco – 'Looking good in print'

Notice how these companies address with a few simple words a promise of something more important being satisfied upon making a positive decision to buy the product or service. There is a promise of a personal outcome being achieved and values being satisfied.

## Why is this important?

If you can attach the fundamental outcomes your customers are looking for when they search out your product or service to any marketing message you create, you will have a much greater influence.

Look at the difference between these approaches to the same thing.

- One hair stylist says come and get your hair cut, the other says come and transform your looks.

- One estate agent says come and buy a house, the other says come and buy a home.

- One bank clerk says open a savings account, the other says plan a secure future.

Which one is more motivational? The one that suggests an important value or outcome being satisfied is automatically more appealing than one that just presents the product or service as it is.

## Your challenge

Your challenge again is to understand and be able to express the important outcomes people want when buying your goods and services. What outcomes do people get satisfied when they buy your service or product? Do you know? How could you find out? People are all different and will have their own reasons for their purchasing decisions. At a higher level, however, certain outcomes and values will resonate with the majority. You need to get to the outcomes that will resonate with the majority of customers you have.

**GREAT QUESTIONS TO ASK POTENTIAL BUYERS – SPECIAL RESPONSE QUESTIONS**

Your buyers are a great source of information and, if you ask them the right questions, you can learn a lot more about what really drives their purchasing decisions.

- What is really important to you when you buy *x*?
- What do you expect when you buy *x*?
- What is the most important thing to you?
- Why do you buy *x*?
- What does buying *x* do for you personally?
- What results do you expect when you buy *x*?
- What is the reason you are making the decision to buy *x*?
- What is personal to you that motivates you to buy *x*?
- What is at the heart of your decision to buy *x*?

## How to use this information

You can use this information to improve your marketing messages, advertising, website copy and your general communication with your customers. The greater your ability to target the exact motivations driving your customers' decisions the quicker you will convert initial interest to a solid sale.

> **Think outcome and motivate more customers to buy**

# 6

# Creating solid foundations

**inspiring ways**
**to market**
**your small business**

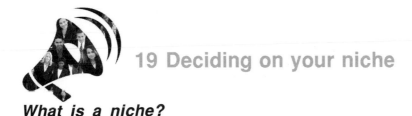

# 19 Deciding on your niche

## What is a niche?

A niche is a specific targeted focus on a pre-selected customer group. A niche can be an area of your expertise or professionalism that you sell to a targeted customer group with a particular demographic profile. It can also be a particular angle you have given to your business that homes in on a specific target customer group with very clear problems that need solving.

## Why do you need a niche?

*'The eagle that chases two rabbits catches neither'*

### You can dominate your portion of the market

It is better not to be a jack of all trades and master of none. Select a niche group of people who you are going to concentrate on as this will give you much more chance of domination within that specific area. You can become the known expert in that niche. It concentrates both your marketing efforts and your expertise.

### People love experts

Experts are seen as people you can trust. If your relationship or marriage was going through a difficult patch and you needed some external help, wouldn't you rather consult an expert on relationships than somebody who practised general counselling? You can feel safer with a specialist.

### Don't spread yourself too thinly

When what you sell potentially can be offered in a different way to a wide selection of people it can result in spreading yourself too thinly. Being too broad can mean that you end up having to work harder to sell yourself and your services. Once you are clear about your niche you will find it a lot easier to explain to people what you do. You will end up facing less competition and if you are good, your name will travel fast.

## *Your challenge*

Selecting a niche does need a lot of thought as it will be the foundation on which your marketing plan will be built. Don't just go with the first idea you think of. Take your time and study your market and customer research.

When you decide on that niche you need to be sure that the niche you choose is one where there is a strong demand. Not only do you need to go fishing where the fish are biting but you also need to go armed with bait to attract them. Once you have found a hungry crowd with a problem you can solve, your only challenge then is to attract them.

## *What makes a niche successful?*

- A niche group of people with a common problem.
- A demand for a solution coupled with the ability and willingness to pay.
- A large enough number of these people to support your business.
- An easy-to-track-down target customer that you can afford to contact.
- Utilising your own personal skills and strengths. If you are good at something you will most likely enjoy it too, which will make it easier to sell.
- Having the experience working within that niche and understand the market place and the people. People like to buy from people who have seen and done it before.
- Others operating within that niche indicating a demand for it.
- Being able to offer something better, different and more appealing.
- Learning from others in the marketplace already working within that niche.
- Finding an opportunity to be an innovator. If there is a low level of competition and there is a market for your products and services, then you are onto a winner.

---

**DECIDING ON YOUR NICHE – SPECIAL RESPONSE CHECKLIST**
*Get some coloured pens and a flip chart and write down your thoughts*
- ▶ Your strengths and skills.
- ▶ Your best and most enjoyable customers to work with.
- ▶ Your broad area of business and expertise.
- ▶ A number of narrower areas you could work in.
- ▶ All you know about the lives and challenges of your customers.
- ▶ Identify customer groups with particular problems.
- ▶ Do your research with these groups to find out what their problems are and what they would buy.
- ▶ Select the five top problems that these groups have.

▶ Describe a number of potential niche groups.
▶ Look and see if they are easy to find. Are they part of an association, club, networking groups? Do they subscribe to particular magazines or publications?
▶ Decide what you could sell them that would solve their problems.

---

**Examples of niches**

A coach who helps people who are facing retirement plan an exciting new life.

A credit control company which helps small business owners get their debtors to pay.

An HR consultant who helps people recently made redundant plan their life change positively.

A financial adviser who helps young people in their first job plan their financial future.

A freelance PA who works virtually with sole proprietors in the retail trade.

A garage which helps local female drivers with their car maintenance problems.

---

## How to use your niche

Once you have your niche you can then start to promote yourself as the expert. Everything you do from now on will be focused on creating the bait that will attract more and more of your niche customers. Your aim will be to become 'famous' for your expertise in this niche. Get people to talk about you and recommend you to others.

> **Think niche and focus**

# 20 Getting clear about what you are selling

## What do you need to be clear about?

Having done your market and customer research and decided on your niche market, the next task is to clarify exactly what it is that you are going to be selling to this market. You will need to be clear about:

- the appropriate products and services
- the appropriate packaging of your products and services
- the appropriate pricing structure.

## Why is it important?

It is vital to be clear about what it is that you are actually selling and the value you are offering. Your communication with your customers will be influenced by your own level of clarity. It is much easier to sell your products and services when you are clear what they are and how they link together. Have you ever not bought from somebody because they were too confusing or offered too much that you just felt overwhelmed. Sometimes less is more. There is a huge marketplace out there and a tremendous amount of choice. So buying from someone who is totally clear about what they have, how it can be of benefit and is able to put that information across in a straightforward manner can be a godsend.

## Your challenge

Be careful of expanding and tailoring your services to suit every customer request that you get. Of course having the flexibility to adapt and package your services in the exact way that your customer requires adds considerable value to your offering, however there must be limit to how much you expand your portfolio of services. If you do simply say yes to every request you get you may end up with a lot of stress and a lot of extra work on your hands. If you are not careful you could end up spending all your time delivering something completely different from what you initially decided to sell. This is fine if it works for you, but not if you have deviated a long way from your core business and are out of your area of expertise.

**HOW TO GET CLEAR ABOUT WHAT YOU ARE SELLING – SPECIAL RESPONSE CHECKLIST**

▶ Study your market, customer and competition research.

▶ Focus on your list of major customer problems that need a solution.

▶ Remind yourself of what it is that your target customers are actually buying from you. Refer to the section in the book 'Understanding what people buy' (Chapter 5).

▶ Look at how your products and services can provide the solution.

▶ Make a list of the appropriate products and services you can offer.

▶ Circle the products and services you want to sell.

▶ Consider how your customers may want to buy these products and services.

▶ Consider ways to package your product and service to facilitate customer choice.

▶ Consider your prices. How do they compare with those of your competitors? Are you charging too much or too little?

▶ Test out some product packages and some prices with your customers.

▶ Listen to feedback from your customers. Notice what people repeatedly ask for or have problems with.

▶ Could you expand your product and service portfolio to accommodate those needs? Make sure you properly assess demand before you jump!


## How to use this information

Once you are clear about exactly what you are selling you are in a position to move forward and create your unique selling proposition, your brand, your strap-line and all your marketing messages. To do this beforehand would be like closing the stable door once the horse has bolted.

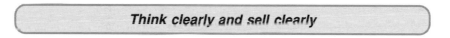

*Think clearly and sell clearly*

# 21 Clarifying your unique selling proposition

## What is a unique selling proposition?

A USP is something that distinguishes you from all your competitors in your local marketplace. It is what makes you so unique that it motivates people to choose you over anyone else. Your USP is a way of stating your unique advantage.

Here are some examples of the USPs of some well known successful businesses, their clever differentiating USPs have helped to propel their respective companies to success.

> Domino's Pizza – *Fresh hot pizza in 30 minutes or less*
> Norwich Union Direct – *We quote you happy*
> Federal Express – *When it absolutely, positively has to be there*

## Why is it important?

It is a competitive marketplace for any small business owner and with many people offering similar products and services you need to do your best to differentiate yourself from the others.

There are many typical statements that businesses make about themselves, open *Yellow Pages* and read some of the adverts in your section. Everybody offers a professional service, quality products and value for money.

Are you saying the same or something different? To stand out you will need to be saying something that is unique and different.

## Your challenge

Your challenge is to identify and communicate your uniqueness and feel completely comfortable when you do. That means you've got to clarify what you do or can start doing for your customers that delivers a result or an advantage that's superior or different from the competition.

This needs to form part of everything you do. You don't just say it, you need to live it, to demonstrate it and to show it. That means whatever you stand for, you do.

Take your time, as your USP is not likely to be the first thing you think of. This needs some careful consideration.

## What makes a USP successful?

Your USP should answer the most fundamental question that every buyer needs to know: 'Why should I buy from you?'

Your USP should communicate the most powerful benefit or advantage you offer to your prospects or customers above your competitors. You must determine what they're not getting from anyone else or what will solve their major fears or frustrations and offer it to them!

Each of these benefits must be:

- Specific and real.
- Measurable (time, quality or quantity).
- Achievable and provable.
- Relevant to your customers' needs and objectives in a positive way.
- Time bound if appropriate.
- Honest and ethical.

### USP DEVELOPMENT – SPECIAL RESPONSE CHECKLIST

- Find out what the main problems or frustrations typical customers have with a product or service similar to yours. Ask people.
- Think about what is special and unique about your business. Make a list.
- Read your testimonials – what positive feedback have you had from your customers?
- What do your satisfied customers repeatedly praise you for?
- Check out your competitors' advertising. Note down the promises they are making.
- Note down what you could offer that is different from the competition.
- Match what you can do particularly well with what problems people want solving.
- Choose a selection of benefits that you could promote that would make your business stand out from the crowd.
- Pick out one or two things that you could make specific and measurable. It may be the speed at which you deliver, the quality you produce, the results you are sure you can deliver. Make sure it passes the SMART test (specific, measurable, achievable, relevant and time bound).
- Test these USPs in your advertising and monitor the response.

## *Sample small business USPs*

Here are some examples of how two companies worked out their potential USPs.

They started with the problems potential customers have and then defined what they wanted instead. USPs easily come to mind as a result of working through this simple process.

---

**Example 1 – website design company**

**Problem** – website design companies can be confusing in their over-technical long-winded explanations which can be hard for non-technical small business owners to understand. They just want to focus on making a success of their marketing and get the job done.

**What customers want** – quick and easy to understand in the first instance – a marketing focus as opposed to a technical one.

USP – A quick, easy, attractive website in a week
USP – The website company that understands small business marketing

---

**Example 2 – Building company**

**Problem** – building companies can be very slow with quotes and proposals following initial visits, and many customers fear that quoted prices can spiral out of control once the job is started. There always seems to be something extra that pops up and/or jobs that tend to take longer than estimated.

**What customers want** – knowledge that the quote will arrive soon after the initial visit enabling decisions to be made. That there is some security in the price quoted and the time estimated to complete the job.

USP – Only three days from visit to quote
USP – The price quoted is the price you pay
USP – We fulfil the completion deadlines we agree

---

## How to use your USP

Once you have put some careful thought into your USP and you have developed it, you will need to integrate it into everything that you do.

Your USP needs to be found in your advertisement headlines, your body copy, in your Yellow Pages adverts. It must find its way to your website home page and be repeated throughout. Your business stationery can even mention of it. When you make a sales presentation or chat at a networking event your USP should always find its way into the conversation. You can never wear it out. If it is good and it works you should shout it from the roof tops.

> **Think USP and find your special something**
> **that customers value most**

# 22 Creating and communicating a brand identity

## What is a brand?

A brand is far more than a snazzy name and a nice bit of artwork. Many people think that a brand is simply the company's logo or corporate identity. It is much more than that.

A brand is the memorable message that is created when a company successfully promotes externally the emotional connection it wants its customers to have with its business.

## Why do you need a brand?

It's not just national businesses that need a brand image. Whatever sized business, club or personality you are, you need to have a clear identity and be memorable in your marketplace. The better your brand image, the more likely you are to sustain business growth and customer support.

## Your challenge

Many businesses have outgrown their image or have one that sends the wrong messages out. If you are a new business you may not have given it any thought at all. Your brand identity and strap-line needs to be a true reflection of your essence and it must communicate instantly with your ideal target audience. It needs to reflect the business you are in and be easy to understand.

This is something you will use throughout your marketing and delivery materials. The more people see it, the more they will remember and associate it with you.

## What makes a brand successful?

Clarity is important. A clear brand message combined with a clear point of difference is the key to success. Your brand image works hand in hand with your unique selling proposition. A successful brand cleverly positions its message and its image to fit with a perceived gap in the marketplace. A gap that people want filled. It then proceeds to maintain that brand value by providing a high level of consistency in both the promotion of and delivery of that value.

**BRAND CREATION – SPECIAL RESPONSE CHECKLIST**

To get this right you will need to focus outwards towards your existing and potential customers; they are the people you want to respond to your brand.

*Step 1 – Research*

▶ Look at other brands in your marketplace – what do you like?

▶ Consider what your current brand communicates to your customers.

▶ Ask your customers what they think.

▶ Ask people who don't use your business currently what they think.

▶ Listen, as perception is reality.

▶ Ask the same customer groups if they were buying a service like yours what their expectations would be.

*Step 2 – Define desired brand values*

▶ Create a list of the values people want from a business like yours.

▶ Brainstorm with your team the values you offer that your customers appreciate.

▶ Choose three or four main values that you would like to Incorporate into your brand.

*Step 3 – See the visual impact you want to create*

▶ Write down words that describe the image you would like to portray to the marketplace.

▶ Find samples of the visual representations of those messages.

▶ Notice the impact of colour – choose colours that hit the right emotional buttons.

▶ Find a designer who listens to exactly what you want to achieve with your brand. Provide a full brief.

*Step 4 – Fine tune with feedback*

▶ Once some sample images have been created, get feedback from a selection of customers and members of the team.

▶ Ask yourself – if I was a customer for this service/product what would this new image communicate to me?

---

**Example**

Five years ago Printinco was known as 'Back up Business Services' hidden away in a small office premises in Wallingford, Oxfordshire. It had inherited an old-fashioned image and a name that did not state clearly what the business was all about.

After conducting some local research to find out what people most wanted from a High Street Print Copy and Design company – the Printinco Brand was created to communicate the following:

- It's obviously print – no confusion.
- It looks good.
- It's modern – with white space and colour.
- It's clean and fresh – this is what your print will look like.
- The quality, professional work a customer would expect.
- A team to serve your needs.

The Printinco business has gone from strength to strength since rebranding and last year opened a second branch in Witney, Oxfordshire. In 2007 Printinco plans to license their trade marked brand image to create a network of operators in the print industry*

> *People will remember your brand when they associate visually with a positive feeling that speaks value*

## How to use your new brand image

Once you have created your brand you will need to make sure that people see it and become familiar with it. Brands become memorable the more they are seen in the marketplace, so you will need to consider a brand awareness campaign. Your brand will be represented on everything you use to communicate with the public. Some useful ways to get your brand out there in the public domain and create awareness are as follows:

- Sponsoring floral displays on roundabouts.
- Bus and transport advertising.
- Banners and signs.
- Bus stop advertising in busy locations.
- Local TV advertising.
- Cinema advertising.
- Sponsoring perimeter boards at local sporting venues.

To make an impact your brand needs to be continually in front of people. You will need to be careful with your advertising budget and choose activities that offer continuity as well as a presence in front of the right people.

> *Think brand and be memorable to your marketplace*

*To view the new Printinco brand image go to www.printinco.co.uk

# 23 Developing a strap-line slogan for your business

## What is a strap-line slogan?

A strap-line slogan is a one line statement about your business that captures the essence of your USP and then positions the value promise that you are making to your customer.

Here are some examples of the strap-line slogans some of the familiar brand names use.

Abbey – *more ideas for your money*
Honda – *the power of dreams*
PC World – *the best of both worlds*
KwikFit – *keeping tyre and exhaust prices down*
Panasonic – *ideas for life*
Tesco – *every little helps*
Dulux – *we know the colours that go*
Shredded Wheat – *put all your heart into life*
Typhoo tea – *you only get an OO with Typhoo*

## Why do you need a strap-line?

People are more likely to remember your name and strap-line slogan than anything else. You can use it to drive a simple, effective message into the minds of your customers which, if done well, will stay there.

## Your challenge

Your challenge is to create exactly the right statement for your business. You must be able to capture the core of what your business is all about in a few simple words, which must be both memorable and inspirational. Words that mean something to your potential customers.

## *To be successful a strap-line must*

- Be memorable.
- Be short and snappy.
- Stand out from the crowd.
- Communicate a value or benefit that ultimately is important to the customer.
- Work with your company name and your logo.
- Speak a language that your audience will relate to.
- Capture the heart of your strength as a business.
- Communicate the heart of your business brand.
- Provoke a positive association.

STRAP-LINE DEVELOPMENT – SPECIAL RESPONSE CHECKLIST

- ▶ Keep in mind the work you have done on your brand image and unique selling proposition in previous chapters.
- ▶ Focus on the reasons why someone may buy from you.
- ▶ Make a list of the values or outcomes they might need satisfying when they buy from you (results, service, pleasure, savings, inspiration, ideas).
- ▶ Write all these words in different coloured pens on a piece of flip chart paper. Put it up on a wall to ponder.
- ▶ Link the words in the list in different combinations.
- ▶ Go for a walk, relax and see what comes up.
- ▶ Test the combinations you have created.
- ▶ Does it communicate a USP?
- ▶ Does it communicate the ultimate value of what you offer to your customers?
- ▶ What does it promise your customers?
- ▶ Is it catchy?
- ▶ How well does it work with your business name and brand image?
- ▶ Leave it for a few days and see whether you have any more inspiration.
- ▶ Test one or two of your ideas with some of your customers and team members.

> **Sample small business strap-lines**
> Occasions Unlimited – *cards and gifts of character*
> Printinco – *looking good in print*
> Haynes Car Care Centre – *ultimate service – economy drive*
> HRworkbench – *powering performance and development*
> Marketingco – *sell more by making your marketing work*
> The Virtual Workshop – *real administrative results*
> Race Energy – *powered by nature – used by people*

## *How to use your strap-line*

You can use your strap-line along with your logo on everything you use to communicate with your customers. It should appear on all your marketing and business literature. It should appear at the end of every email that you send out. It needs to appear in your advertising and on your website.

This is a message that you want people to associate with you and your business, so whenever you get the opportunity to use it – do it!

> **Think strap-line slogan and capture the value you offer**

## 24 Believing in yourself

### What is self-belief?

Self-belief is a feeling of confidence in your own values, skills and experiences. It is a voice inside your head that says I can do this. It is a sense of knowing yourself and what you are capable of. It is looking at yourself and what you stand for positively. Having self-belief doesn't mean that you are perfect. Believing in yourself often means that you accept your weaknesses whilst seeing your strengths at the same time. Having self-belief means you can be honest with yourself, make mistakes and learn from them, be realistic. You don't get knocked back by others' comments or opinions. You are steadfast in your approaches, consistent. You know deep down you can do this.

### Why is it important?

If you have taken that enormous leap of faith and started your own business then you must have bucket loads of self-belief already. You do need to maintain it. Running your own business is completely different from life in the corporate world. Everything relies on you. To be a success and do yourself and your business justice you need to maintain your self-belief.

### Your challenge

Everybody has moments of doubt or can be unsure about something or other from time to time; it is a natural process. The challenge is not to let those moments accumulate and affect your self-belief. You will always face the challenge of other people's comments and opinion. You may have noticed in your life that there are people that you feel good being around and others you don't. Some people give you positive energy because they believe in you. You feel it and you rise to the occasion. Others may always have a negative comment to make about what you are doing or talking about. Don't let these comments rock your self-belief. Always question the person's reason for the comment. If it is based on fact you will listen; if not, then it is only their opinion. You will need to stay strong.

**HOW TO BELIEVE IN YOURSELF – SPECIAL RESPONSE CHECKLIST**

To develop a high level of self-belief these are some of the things that you can do.

▶ Make a list of all the things that you are good at.

▶ Keep a record of all the positive comments made about you or the service you offer and read them from time to time.

▶ Relive experiences when you have relied on yourself and made a success of something. It could be anything from achieving in a sporting event, travel, going to college or university, getting your first job.

▶ Think about times when you have overcome adversity. What did you do? What qualities did this demonstrate?

▶ What do you think you do really well in the business that you are in?

▶ Talk yourself up. Monitor the way you talk to yourself. Say I can more often than I can't.

▶ Look at what you have achieved as opposed to what you haven't.

## How to use this information

Just be aware of your own varying levels of self-belief and how this is impacting on you and your business. Take as many opportunities to build yourself up. The stronger your self-belief is the more likely you will be to succeed.

> **Think 'I am the best' and you will be**

# Getting the price right

**inspiring ways
to market
your small business**

# 25 Charging what you are worth

This section is focused on pricing a service-related business as opposed to pricing products.

## What are you worth?

Pricing can be the most complex part of the whole marketing process. What are you worth? What is your service worth? How do you justify your rates or prices? There is a lot to think about. The most important thing to consider about prices and rates is that you must charge in accordance with the value that your client will receive from you. To find out what you need to charge you must start by establishing what you are worth in terms of the value you give your clients.

Your service or skill will be more valuable if:

- you can solve a very costly problem and save your customer money
- you add tangible and solid value to your buyer's bottom line
- what you do is rare or in demand and there is a shortage of suppliers
- you can offer value that no-one else can
- you have a history of success and results achievement that back you up
- you have a strong unconditional guarantee.

## Why is it important to charge what you are worth?

Pricing can be a strange thing. It has a strong influence on how you feel about the value of what you do. If you undercharge you may end up working very hard for not a lot. You may be perceived as cheap and therefore not so valuable. You may end up with a lot of work but no time to develop and grow your business or your skills. You may get stuck at a level that you find hard to raise. Over-charging can be equally problematic. You may price yourself out of the market, or find yourself under such intense pressure to deliver the high value that equates to the price you are charging that it affects your delivery. Either way it is important to find the right balance both for you and for your customers. You need to feel comfortable about the price you charge your customers and your customers must feel comfortable about the value they perceive themselves to be receiving.

## *Your challenge*

Your challenge will be to establish your worth to your customers and put a price on it. You will then need to communicate the value you are offering to justify that price. You will need to decide exactly how you are going to price your work, i.e.

- by the hour
- by the project
- by the package
- by the solution
- by results.

People's perception of the price you charge can also be a challenge for you.

It is important to recognise that how your product or service is perceived is largely determined by what price you charge for it. Perception of price can influence both buying and selling behaviours. Some only see the value when the price is high, and if low the assumption can be that the quality is absent.

**WHAT IS YOUR PERCEPTION OF PRICE? – SPECIAL RESPONSE CHECKLIST**
- ▶ How do you feel when you deliver the highest price for your goods and services?
- ▶ How do you feel when you deliver the lowest?
- ▶ How quickly do you discount?
- ▶ Why do you discount prices?
- ▶ When you present your price, are there differences in how you react to different customers?
- ▶ If there are, what are the reasons for that?
- ▶ How do you think about money? What are some of your beliefs?
- ▶ When you make purchases, is price the most important thing to you?
- ▶ If it is not the most important thing, what is?

Most people think their perception is reality. It is not. Being able to challenge your own perception is useful if you want to be able to ask for the best price for your goods or services more of the time. Being aware of your client's perception of price is useful too. You will be able to recognise those people who are more concerned about the value they are getting, than what is on the price tag. Don't let your own beliefs about money get in the way of your customers spending theirs.

## *How do you know what to charge?*

There are many aspects you will need to consider.

- The potential value of each project to each client
- The potential impact the solution will have on your client's bottom line
- What the market conditions are in your industry
- What your competitors charge versus what they offer
- The time it will take to complete the project
- The complexity of the project
- The client's timescales
- The resources required to deliver the results

**IS YOUR PRICE RIGHT – SPECIAL RESPONSE CHECKLIST**

- What do you charge?
- How much do your prices vary?
- Why do you charge the prices you do?
- How do you work out your prices?
- Do you feel your prices are a true reflection of your value to your customer?
- Could you charge more?
- If so, how would you justify the price?
- Could you charge in a different way (by the project, solution or result)?
- What impact would charging in a different way have?
- How could you test it?

## *How to use this information*

Questioning your own pricing structure and the way it is presented to your clients is a very useful exercise. Develop a value pricing strategy. Consider ways to add value to your service that will justify the prices you want to charge. Look for a way to increase your prices and make a positive impact on your bottom line.

> **Think value before price**

## 26 Increasing prices at the right time

If you increase your prices you can increase your profit margins. The question is can you do that? People do not buy on price alone and if you raised your prices what impact could it have on the business that you do?

If you raised your prices you may be able to afford to do some of the things that would add value to your service and make you stand out from the crowd.

Raising prices might result in you losing the bottom end of your customer base. You may want to lose this bottom end because it contains low-priced jobs that take time and effort to service. It may be preferable to go up-market and do less for more. Increasing prices may only affect some of the business that you have; others may not even notice. Think about your local restaurant, if they raised the price of your favourite main course dish from £10.50 to £11.75 would you stop ordering it?

### *Why is timing important?*

If you are going to raise your prices, doing it in the right way at the right time is important. Your loyal regular customers will need advance warning of any price rises ensuring that they are not taken by surprise.

You will also need to consider the impact of financial year ends to make sure that any price increases happen before budgeting periods. It is best to make it as easy as possible for your existing customers to adapt to those price increases.

How and when you raise your prices will depend on the type of business you are in. A retail business for example could raise its prices any time, whereas a trade or manufacturing business which supplies products for resale would need to plan ahead and choose the right time for their customers.

New year or at the start of your financial year can be a good time to move forward with price increases. Following a sale, introducing new stock, a refurbishment or a move to new premises can be triggers to raise prices. If you can show your customers that you have raised your game as well as your prices and are now offering more value than you were before, it will make it easier for any changes to be accepted.

## *What is the right increase to make?*

This will depend on a number of important factors.

- What you want to achieve with your price increase.
- How much will or will not influence business.
- What additional value you are able to offer to justify the price.
- Market conditions.
- What your competitors are doing.

**SHOULD YOU INCREASE YOUR PRICES – SPECIAL RESPONSE CHECKLIST**

- ▶ Could you increase your prices?
- ▶ What would you want to achieve by it?
- ▶ What impact would raising your prices by 10% have on your business?
- ▶ When would be the best time to do this?
- ▶ What additional value could you offer to justify the price increase?
- ▶ How would you communicate this to your customers?

## *How to use this information*

People don't usually buy on price and if they do they don't always get the value they anticipated. Many people don't even notice the price. Consider where you could charge more for what you offer and try it. Enjoy the positive impact it has on you and your business.

> **Think price increase and increase profit**

# 8

# Developing your marketing message

**inspiring ways
to market
your small business**

# 27 Creating commitments to your customers

## What is a commitment statement?

A commitment statement is a simple expression of the promises you make to your customers about what you are going to do for them if they use your service. A commitment statement will normally be no more than one page of clearly articulated points about your business and the value you offer. It could be expressed in any number of different ways. Here are some example headline introductions.

- The secrets of *x* Business's great service.
- The top ten reasons to use *x*.
- The seven reasons our customers love us.
- Our special commitments to you are...

## Why is it important?

It is important to capture the essence of what you offer your customers. Business owners often walk on water for their customers but never tell a soul about it. Your commitment statement is a way of communicating all that is really special about your service. Your statement will highlight what matters to your customers and is most likely to motivate them to buy from you. Once you have articulated and communicated your promises, consistent delivery is vital.

## Your challenge

Your challenge will be to dig deep and find out what your commitments actually are in the real world. Your satisfied customers know what they are, but do you? You can be so close to your own business that you can end up taking the things you do for your customers for granted.

Your challenge will be to extract from the people that use your service what it is that they really value. You will need to recall conversations with customers when they appeared particularly pleased with something you did for them. Find testimonials and thank you letters and read them. Notice what stands out. Remind yourself of some of the problems your customers have had and how specifically your service has provided the solution.

## What makes a commitment statement successful?

Your commitment statement must be genuine and expressed in a way that ensures your customers believe in you. Each statement needs to be honest, real, deliverable and meaningful to your customers. You must convey value quickly and simply. Your commitments should solve problems for your customers and provide answers to the questions they have inside their heads before they buy from you.

Your customers need to be able to look over your list of commitments and think 'yes' I want to do business with these people. If they do that, then you have been successful.

**Sample commitment statements**
Car service garage with onsite car parts retail outlet

**The secrets of $x$'s great service.**
- We are completely honest and truthful with you.
- We find solutions for your individual vehicle problems.
- Our knowledge of what is required can save you money.
- You get a quick and simple explanation.
- If we haven't got the part we will source it or make it.
- All car parts are tried and tested so we know they work.
- We deliver to our trade customers quickly.
- Car service – we will pick you up and drop you home locally.
- If you need help at short notice – we jump!
- You get modern technology with old fashioned values.
- You can rely on us 110%.
- We care about doing our absolute best for you.

A virtual personal assistant

**Seven good reasons to use our service.**
- We set you free from the paperwork pile.
- You get the expertise of an experienced PA at a fraction of the cost.
- We do the detail – you do what you are good at.
- We keep the high standards that your customers expect.
- As perfectionists getting your job done right is a must.
- We listen and respond to your priorities.
- We always seek the best solution for you.

**CREATING A COMMITMENT STATEMENT – SPECIAL RESPONSE CHECKLIST**

▶ Make a list of all the special things you do for your customers that you don't tell anyone about.

▶ Ask your staff to do the same.

▶ Choose some of your best regular customers and conduct a short telephone survey. Choose a person to conduct the survey who is able to extract from your customers the essence of what motivates them to use your business. Here are some sample questions:

1. What do you expect when you use a service like ours?
2. What would make it exceptional in your opinion?
3. What are some of the reasons you use our service?
4. What motivated you to use our service in the first place?
5. What problems have we solved for you?
6. What do you think we do really well?
7. In terms of continuing to use a service like ours, what is most important to you?

▶ Use this information to create a list of up to ten major benefits.

▶ Be succinct and honest.

## How to use this information

Once created you can integrate your customer commitment statement into your

- website
- sales brochure
- sales letter
- post sales package
- banners or posters at exhibitions
- sales conversations with customers.

> **Think customer commitment statement
> and shout about your values**

# 28 Developing an elevator speech

## What is an elevator speech?

An elevator speech is you talking about your business in public in an inspirational way. To elevate means to raise or lift higher and this is what this speech is all about. You may be talking for one minute or longer at a networking event, introducing yourself to business colleagues, or giving your opening speech at the start of a presentation. An elevator speech should build you and your business up and motivate your audience to want find out more.

## Why is having one important?

There are many opportunities to talk about your business with others. If you want to inspire sales then you need to get used to talking yourself and your business up. Once you are confident with the content of your elevator speech it can be a relief. You will know what to say in any situation when you are asked to describe what you do.

## Your challenge

Do you find describing what you do difficult? Is building your business up in a positive way even harder? What is it that you find challenging? It can be hard to be succinct and powerful at the same time, especially when you know your own business well. It can be overwhelming when there is so much that you do. How do you choose what to say? Selecting exactly the right words and delivering them with passion and enthusiasm is the challenge. Knowing your business is very different from selling your business.

## What makes an elevator speech successful?

How your elevator speech impacts on those listening is the most important thing. Your aim is to capture attention and build in your audience a desire to make contact with you. Your speech needs to communicate very quickly the essence of what you do and the value you offer. It must be relevant to and motivational for your audience. You must be fluent and believe fully in what you are saying.

**ELEVATOR CREATOR – SPECIAL RESPONSE CHECKLIST**

To create your elevator speech, get a pen and paper and write down your answers to the following set of questions.

- ▶ Who are you talking to?
- ▶ What are their interests/problems/needs?
- ▶ What aspect of what you do could be of most interest to them?
- ▶ What can you do to solve these problems?
- ▶ What is the best thing about your service?
- ▶ What is your USP?
- ▶ What have those that use your service said about it?
- ▶ What is your guarantee?
- ▶ What action would you like people to take as a result of listening to your elevator speech?

## How to use this information

Take this information and use it to write your speech. Here is a simple structure to follow:

- I am ... and my company is ...
- Thank you for the opportunity to speak.
- We help people (describe target customer) who (describe typical problems these customers face).
- We help these people to (describe solutions to problems).
- The best thing about our business is ...
- We are unique in ...
- Those who have used us say that they appreciate our ...
- When we work with people we guarantee ...
- If you are interested in finding out more (action to take).

Your speech can now be used at any event where you get the opportunity to blow your own trumpet. Deliver it with honesty and sincerity and you cannot fail to inspire your audience.

## 29 Creating a guarantee

### What is a guarantee?

A guarantee is an offer you make to your customers that reduces or takes away the perceived risk of making a purchase. When anyone decides not to buy your product or service their perceived risk may be

- making the wrong decision
- losing money
- not receiving what they have paid for
- not being satisfied and then not being able to get their money back.

### Why is a guarantee important?

Whilst these perceived fears may be overcome during your sales presentation or consultation process, the offer of a rock solid guarantee can give your customer the security they need to go ahead sooner rather than later. A guarantee can make it less threatening to consider your offer. The right guarantee can motivate a potential customer to take the risk as opposed to consider it. This can dramatically increase the speed of your sales cycle. Typically an unsatisfied customer tells nine people about their experience but with a guarantee that gives an unsatisfied customer an immediate get-out, this can be dramatically reduced.

### Your challenge

Your challenge is to embrace a strong guarantee. Do not be afraid to offer the best promise that you can live up to. The chances are that hardly any customers will take you up on it. Think about how often any of your existing customers have asked for their money back or complained.

### What makes a guarantee successful?

A strong guarantee can draw attention to your confidence in your product or service. If it is really powerful it can inspire action. It needs to be a guarantee that you are completely comfortable delivering. It needs to completely take away any perceived risks of purchase. It needs to demonstrate full confidence in your service. It should be specific and include full claim details. It needs to be both meaningful and measurable.

Your guarantee could be your unique selling proposition and attract a lot of attention to your business.

---

**Sample guarantees**

Internet based survey software company offers you the opportunity to try their service free of charge for a full 30 days completely free of charge.

Business growth workshop – guarantees to refund the full 100% course fee at lunch time on day two if not completely satisfied.

Business consultant guarantees to pay his consultancy fees back in full if his clients do not make an additional £12,000 within 12 months of using his service and implementing the actions set.

A company selling e-books and CDs guarantees full 100% money back in addition to allowing you to keep the products.

---

**GUARANTEE CREATOR – SPECIAL RESPONSE CHECKLIST**

▶ Look at your competitors' guarantees and note down any really good ones.
▶ Guarantee strengths. What do you do particularly well that you know your customers value. Would you be able to guarantee any of it 100%.
▶ Guarantee results. Look at all the problems your customers want solutions to. What are the results that are most important to them? Could you guarantee any of these results?
▶ Choose a financial payback that has high perceived customer value. Could you exceed even the 100% money back guarantee and offer to compensate them for their time and effort in going through the buying process with you.
▶ Consider how you could make your guarantee memorable.

## How to use this information

Your guarantee can be one of your most powerful marketing tools. Once you have created one you think has impact you need to test it. Measure its impact on your conversion rate. Integrate your guarantee into every piece of sales and marketing literature you have.

How you word your guarantee will make all the difference. Here are some strong words and phrases that will add some power to the communication of it.

- Unconditional money back guarantee.
- We stand behind our promise of . . .
- My 110% 'call me crazy' guarantee.
- Absolutely no risk to you.
- 100% no hassle, no-questions-asked refund.
- I personally guarantee.
- 100% on the spot refund.
- Better than risk free.

> **Think guarantee and take away buyers' reservation**

# Determining your
# marketing methods

**inspiring ways
to market
your small business**

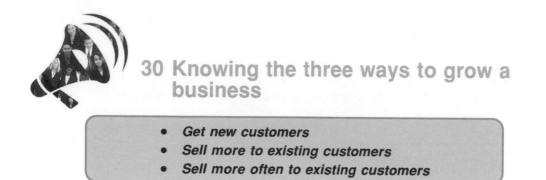

# 30 Knowing the three ways to grow a business

- *Get new customers*
- *Sell more to existing customers*
- *Sell more often to existing customers*

To grow any business you will need to either attract new customers or increase transaction value and frequency of purchase of the customers you have already got. Or even better you can do all three.

If you were the owner of a baker's shop one way to sell more would be to attract more customers. You could do this by offering a free loaf to every new customer. Another way would be to sell more to the customers you have got. You could offer a special meal deal that consists of a baguette, a cake, a packet of crisps and a drink at a special package price. A third way would be to encourage the customers you have got to come in and shop more frequently. You could do that by creating a loyalty card and giving discounts for frequent visits.

## Why is this information important?

Many people focus on getting new customers as if this was the only way to build business. This is in fact the most costly and time-consuming route to more business. Building business with existing customers by creating ways for them to buy more and more often is a far cheaper and quicker way to increase revenues and ultimately profits.

## Your challenge

Your challenge is to know your figures and to open your mind to ways to develop each of the three ways to grow any business.

## The dimensions of business growth

Your total business revenue will be made up out of the number of customers you have, multiplied by the amount they spend, multiplied by how often they spend it.

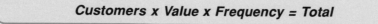

*Customers x Value x Frequency = Total*

**Example**

If you have ten customers who spend £1,000 twice a year your total revenue will be £20,000.

If you get one new customer and get those 11 customers to spend 10% more three times a year you will see your revenues reach £36,300.

If you get five extra customers and encourage all 15 to spend 50% more four times a year you will be looking at a cool £90,000.

And finally if you manage to double your number of customers to 20, double their spend and increase the number of times they buy from you to five times a year, you will increase your turnover from £20,000 to £200,000.

### CHECK YOUR OWN DIMENSIONS OF BUSINESS GROWTH – SPECIAL RESPONSE QUESTIONS

- How many customers do you have right now?
- How much do they spend in an average transaction with you?
- How many times a year do they spend this with you?
- What would happen if you increased these figures by 5%, 10%, 20% or 50%?
- What ideas do you have that could increase transaction value?
- What ideas do you have that could increase frequency of purchase?

## How to use this information

Evaluate some of the tactics for boosting business with existing customers and attracting new customers. Choose the best to integrate into your business and you can expect to see a measurable impact on your bottom line.

> *Think three ways to grow and maximise*
> *your business potential*

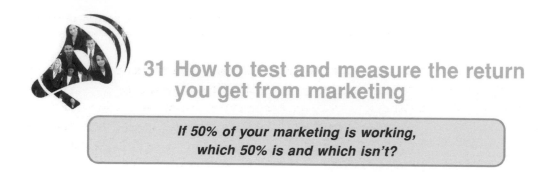

# 31 How to test and measure the return you get from marketing

> *If 50% of your marketing is working,*
> *which 50% is and which isn't?*

## What is testing and measuring?

Testing and measuring means finding out what specific results you are getting from the marketing activities you engage in. It is about generating some tangible facts and figures to support your future marketing plans. It will enable you to go beyond gut feel or 'suck it and see'. By testing and measuring you will create the figures, the sales results and the numbers to support your marketing proposals.

## Why is it important?

Do you know for sure which of your current marketing methods work the best? Can you tell where the majority of your new enquiries come from? Do you know how much of your product or service you sold as a direct result of a particular advertising campaign? If you do not have this information you have no way of learning about your business or your customers' responses to your marketing activities. How can you fine tune your delivery to improve results if you don't know what they are in the first place? How can you make decisions about where to spend your budget year on year? How can you decide what to drop and what to repeat? Testing and measuring the specific results you get from marketing is absolutely necessary if you want to evaluate your return on any investment you make.

## Your challenge

Your challenge will be setting up a system to test and measure each of your marketing activities. You will need the discipline to work your system until you have gathered enough information to come to meaningful conclusions. Don't give up before you have had a chance to test and measure thoroughly. It will be worth it in the long run. You will save time, money and effort by ultimately focusing on what works and stop wasting money on what doesn't.

Some marketing methods will be harder to test than others. Direct response marketing like advertising, direct mail, email campaigns and telesales campaigns are easier to test and measure than general brand awareness marketing like poster campaigns, transport advertising and billboards. To come to a buying decision customers may have come into contact with a number of your marketing messages over a period of time before a positive response is triggered.

## What makes testing and measuring successful?

Testing and measuring needs to be systematic. You need to decide how each method will be tested and measured prior to starting. You will also need a system of recording the information. A simple spreadsheet can be an easy way to do this.

## Test on a smaller scale first

If you are planning a direct mail campaign, test a smaller number on a targeted group and count up the responses you get before you send out the larger batch. If it doesn't work well enough you will have a chance to fine tune the approach, then try a different headline or a different offer.

## Get team understanding and support

If you have a team of people working in your business it is likely that they will be involved in gathering customer response information. The more they understand about the importance of finding out what is working and what isn't the more likely they will be to follow through with the system necessary to get it right.

## Choose the right measure for the right method

Make your measures creative and different. You may make a specific offer in one advert. You might have a particular response process that applies to a sales campaign that enables you to track the results. You could propose an outrageous freebie in a local directory listing. You may set up different codes or reply references on email campaigns. You may have signed up to a website traffic report. The measure will need to be appropriate to the marketing method used and easy to monitor.

## Ask people where they heard about you

Asking people where they heard about your business is probably the easiest and most instant way to get answers. Get everybody in your organisation to gather this information. It can be done on the telephone when you get an enquiry. It can be asked in conversation or at the end of a customer transaction. This information needs to be recorded, collated and evaluated.

**YOUR TEST AND MEASURE – SPECIAL RESPONSE CHECKLIST**
- ▶ What marketing methods are you using at the moment?
- ▶ How are you testing and measuring the return you get?
- ▶ Do you know what is working best?
- ▶ If not, what could you do to introduce relevant measures?
- ▶ How could you systemise your testing and measuring process?
- ▶ Decide on what you can test and measure.
- ▶ How you are going to do it?
- ▶ How and who is going to record the information?
- ▶ Review results and make decisions.

## How to use this information

The information must be used to optimise the return you get from your marketing. Cut out those methods that do not work after thoroughly testing and fine tuning. Use more of the methods that work by doing everything you can to maximise impact.

For example if your window display is one of the most popular customer magnets, then make the most of it. Change the display, promote special offers, use it to introduce new products. Keep it clean and clear. Use testing and measuring to support continuous learning about your marketing and your customers' responses.

> *Think test and measure and find out*
> *what works and what doesn't*

# 32 Choosing the best methods to market your business

## What are the best methods?

The best methods to market your business are those that enable you to target the right people with the right message and gain the greatest return on your investment.

## Why is it important to analyse the right methods for your business?

There are so many methods out there in the marketplace to choose from that you could be overwhelmed with information and possibilities. There is a lot to learn about how each method works and what is involved in getting it set up. It is important to understand and appreciate how each method could form a vital part of your marketing strategy before you make big decisions about how you spend your marketing budget. Poor decisions can result in a lot of wasted time and effort.

## Your challenge

Your challenge will be to avoid getting overloaded with information and allowing that to stop you taking action. Paralysis by analysis can be a problem for many. Find quick and easy ways of exploring the potential of the marketing methods that could be ideal for your business. This book is designed to give you the essentials, enabling you to move forward swiftly to create a strategy that has the best chance of working for you.

YOUR BEST METHOD SELECTION CRITERIA – SPECIAL RESPONSE CHECKLIST
When evaluating any potential marketing method you can check out its viability by running it through this checklist.

- ▶ What is the method?
- ▶ What do you know about it?
- ▶ What marketing goals do you expect this method will help you to achieve?
- ▶ What other business similar to yours has used this method and got results?
- ▶ Can you find this out?
- ▶ What kind of result is it possible to achieve?
- ▶ What are the potential benefits for a business like yours?

▶ Is there any guarantee of success?

▶ What are the risks involved?

▶ What resources, investment and time are required to get it set up?

▶ Have you got the resources and time to set up and run this marketing method?

▶ What will it cost you in terms of time and money to do this?

▶ How will you measure your success?

## How to use this information

Read this book and take note of any of the methods that you think could work for your business. Run each you choose through this checklist before you add it to your marketing plan.

> **Think best method and make the best choices**

# 33 Being creative with your ideas

## What does being creative mean?

Being creative is all about your ability to come up with ways of doing things differently. It is about thinking outside of normal boundaries and rules, thinking outside of the box that the majority stay within. Creative thinkers use more of their right brain which is that part of your brain that accesses ideas and concepts, as opposed to their left brain which controls logic and order. We can all be creative if we allow ourselves to be and being good at marketing your business will need you to develop ways to capture the spirit of your business and stand out from the crowd.

## Why is it important?

With the persistent competition for market share and the ever increasing pressure to do things better, cheaper and quicker in order to stand a chance of success, creative thinking is a must. If you can, come up with innovative ways of promoting yourself you will be remembered when others are forgotten. It is often easier to follow the crowd in any industry, to do something because it is expected or because it has always been done that way. It takes courage to break free and be different. Good creative ideas can propel you forward and help you to stimulate the mind of your customer.

## Your challenge

Some business owners would not describe themselves as being creative. This is probably because they have never really allowed themselves to be. By creating the right circumstances and allowing your mind to run free we all have the potential for bright ideas. Being creative is all about opening your mind to possibilities and letting go of the reins of control. Most of us come up with our best ideas when we are relaxed, enjoying ourselves or being stimulated by a new environment. It is hardest to be creative when you are walking the treadmill of familiar daily tasks. Your greatest challenge will be to create opportunities to let your mind relax giving it a chance to get stimulated outside of a normal routine environment.

**Creative marketing ideas – small business examples**

Here are some good examples of how some small businesses have used their creative minds to come up with different ways of generating new leads and interest in their businesses.

A new hair salon wanted to get more attention in their city centre location to drive new customers to book appointments and to collect contact details for their customer database. Thinking outside the box and utilising the resources they had they came up with the idea of running a hair styling competition for the stylists at their salon, the results of which were modelled and voted on in the city centre on a busy Saturday. Shoppers who voted had to complete an entry form which allowed those who voted for the winning style entry into a draw to win a free makeover at the salon. The entry form included full contact details which enabled all those who took part to be mailed a special thank you voucher giving discounts on hair appointments. They achieved free press coverage both advertising for the models to take part and the event itself. Their stylists got some good exposure as well as generating entertainment and interest for shoppers on a Saturday.

A retail outlet selling teddy bears and a range of soft toys wanted to encourage more families with children to visit their shop. They wanted to communicate fun and excitement and to drive the right people to their door. They came up with the idea of running a hunt the bears competition. They took picture of all their top bears and gave them all a special name. They arranged to put pictures of the bears up in different places in the town centre. To enter the competition, families had to complete an entry form that requested contact details. The competition involved correctly matching the named bears with a location. All correct entries were entered into a draw to win the bear of their choice. Competition entry forms had to be delivered to the shop where entrants were given a special gift voucher. This creative marketing idea generated a lot of fun and attracted a crowd of excited kids who all wanted a bear.

An Indian restaurant promoted its special lunchtime menu by offering a tray of tempting sample dishes at a local riverside event which was taking place only five minutes' walk from their restaurant.

A ball gown specialist who wanted to target the local student market advertised for aspiring student models and ran a free fashion show and modelling competition at one of the universities. Students voted for both the best model and the best gown. The winner wearing the chosen gown got their picture in the local newspaper along with an excellent write-up about the event.

## How to be creative – special response checklist

▶ Where are you when you find you come up with your best ideas? Go there more often.

▶ Have you tried a creative marketing ideas brainstorming session with your team?

▶ Take your team out of the office and just let your minds run free: all ideas are accepted no matter how crazy. If you create an environment that is free from criticism and analysis you will be amazed at what comes up.

▶ Some of the reality business programmes on television like *Risking It All, The Apprentice, Dragons' Den* are great for stimulating ideas. If you see something you like, think about how you could apply it to your business in a different way.

▶ What kind of fun creative activity do you think would get your business some attention?

▶ What kind of competition could you run?

▶ What could you do that would attract some positive press coverage?

▶ What could you do that is different and unique?

▶ Get yourself a brightly coloured artist's pad and some coloured pens. Help yourself think creatively by drawing and linking ideas together. Mind maps are a useful way of connecting your ideas and allowing one thought to branch off into another.

▶ Keep a record of your ideas whenever they occur to you and let them develop.

▶ What could you do that would really communicate the spirit of your business?

## How to use this information

When you come up with a new and different approach to the marketing or advertising of your business make sure that it has the best chance of attracting the right people and giving out the right message about your business. Keep your eye on your brand image and make sure that anything you do is supportive of it. If your idea ticks all the right boxes give it a try and just like any other marketing method you use it will need to be tested and measured.

> *Think outside the box and stand out from the crowd*

# 10

# Marketing methods that boost business with existing customers

**inspiring ways
to market
your small business**

# 34 Communicating with your existing customers

## *What is a communication system?*

A communication system is a planned series of activities that ensure that you keep in constant communication with your existing customers. Elements of a communication system could include a monthly e-newsletter, new product or service alerts emails, an annual or biannual customer review meeting, an invitation to a special event or hospitality day, Christmas cards and gifts, free tickets to events, a golf day, day at the races, free useful information or learning opportunity.

## *Why is it important?*

When you first get a new customer there is usually a lot of energy and enthusiasm. Your customer has made a decision to use you because they believe that you will provide the solution they are looking for. You are keen to deliver and pleased because you have successfully attracted a new customer to your business. This is where the relationship starts. There are many factors that will influence the length of time that customer is active with you. The longer you can keep that customer an enthusiastic purchaser the stronger your business will be.

A well-planned communication system will help to keep your customers focused on you and what you have to offer them. It will help you to retain customers.

A communication system can also help you to bring back inactive customers or those who have been customers but, for whatever reason, have stopped doing business with you. It will help you to reduce attrition.

There are some interesting statistics that show the main reasons why business is lost and their relative percentages.

- 1% of customers died
- 3% moved out of the area
- 5% were influenced away
- 9% got a better deal
- 14% because of unresolved conflicts
- 68% left because of perceived indifference i.e. apathy or lack of communication.

By nurturing your customers from the start and maintaining the communication and the relationship, you will avoid losing the 68% who stop using you because of perceived indifference. This could have a significant effect on your sales results.

## Your challenge

Your challenge will be to develop and deliver a system of customer communication that adds value to your relationships. Communicating with customers is a balancing act. People do not want to be bombarded with information day in day out. They don't want to be overwhelmed by so many invitations and gifts that they have to keep saying no. They don't want to buy one thing from you and find that suddenly they are being forced to contend with more and more offers of products and services that they really don't need. You know from your own experience what this can be like. You will need to create a communication system that appreciates your customers' situation and maintains rapport.

## What makes a communication system successful?

- It is set up with the customer in mind first and foremost.
- It offers the customer added value.
- You surprise and delight your customers from time to time and show appreciation for the business that they do with you.
- It is focused on building a greater rapport.
- You regularly ask for feedback and are prepared to fine tune your system.
- When you have details of the personal interests of your best customers you tailor your offers of events and information to suit them.

### COMMUNICATION SYSTEM – SPECIAL RESPONSE CHECKLIST

- ▶ Decide what you want your communication system to achieve for you.
- ▶ Be aware of the level of attrition (customers who stop using you) that is experienced in your business.
- ▶ Understand why people stop doing business with you.
- ▶ Do you want to continue to work with those who have stopped doing business with you?
- ▶ What could you do to re-contact those people who have stopped using your service?
- ▶ Find out as much as you can about your key customers' interests.

▶ Be aware of special events coming up for any of your customers that are important to them such as a shop opening, business anniversary or winning an award. Simple congratulations or good luck cards will always be appreciated.

▶ What kind of special events, days out, tickets or information would these people potentially be interested in?

▶ What could you do once a year that would be appreciated by your customers?

## *How to use this information*

The following chapters will give you more details about what you could include in your communication system. A well-organised customer database management process will help to make this whole process easier for you to implement and manage on an ongoing basis.

> **Think customer communication and keep the connection**

# 35 Building trusting relationships

## What is a trusting relationship?

A trusting relationship is built when your customers feel connected with you as a person and confident that you have their interests and needs at heart. You will be their first choice when they have a relevant problem that needs solving. Trust is built up over time and through experiences. If you have always maintained a level of service that delivers exactly what has been promised, you do what you say you are going to do and your customer is completely satisfied then it will be easy to build trust. Trust is about integrity and values. It matters deeply to people and is very personal.

## Why is trust an important relationship ingredient?

Trusting relationships form the backbone of successful businesses. In a world where there is a lot of choice people will always support those that they trust the most. Customers are actually looking to build trust. They want it. It builds buyers' security. Trust is a high value for many. If the trust is there then customers will listen to your advice, make decisions based on your suggested solutions and often not question your prices as much as they would if they were unsure of you. Building trusting relationships can help you to retain customers, gain customers and increase the amount of referrals that you get.

## Your challenge

Depending on the nature of your business you will no doubt come into contact with a lot of people. You will need to work hard to maintain your standards and make sure that however brief your contact is with each individual, it is positive. Small things can break trust in an instant: not getting a proposal or a telephone follow up you have promised done in time; a sharp word when you are tired or stressed, forgetting a name, an important detail about a business or worse making silly mistakes that affect your customer's belief in your service. Trust can take a long time to build and an instant to break.

## What builds trust in relationships?

- Demonstrating a natural respect for people.
- Asking questions and really listening to what people want.

- Showing you understand what matters to each individual.
- Being honest, even if it means that you do not sell your services.
- Giving ideas and advice away for free.
- Delivering whatever you promise.
- Letting people know if for any reason you cannot deliver.
- Doing the best you can for people.
- Being genuine.
- Time and contact.

**YOUR EXISTING CUSTOMER RELATIONSHIP – SPECIAL RESPONSE CHECKLIST**

Consider the level of trust that you have with your existing customers. Ask yourself the following questions and be honest in answering them.

- How do you know if a customer trusts you?
- Name the customers you have with whom you think you have a trusting relationship.
- What is the difference between those with whom you have a trusting relationship and those you don't?
- How do you build trust with people?
- What could you do to build more trust?

## How to use this information

Be conscious of the trust you have with the people you do business with. Notice the signs. Work harder to both build it and maintain it. It will be worth it.

> *Think build trust and build business*

# 36 Reviewing customers' needs

## What do customers need?

The reason a person became a customer of yours the first time may not be the same reason that they continue to buy from you in the future. Existing customers have changing needs the same as any new potential customer would. They need ongoing understanding and communication.

## Why is understanding them important?

Taking the time to understand what your existing customers' changing needs might be will ensure that you are right there with answers before they think of using anyone else. It is important that you keep talking to your customers as they are a great source of information for you. Their changing needs can be representative of market demand which could influence the longer term development plans for your product or service. Taking the time to find out what your existing customers' needs are likely to be in the future could give you business development ideas. Taking your existing customers' business for granted without reviewing their needs could be dangerous. Do they know about the full range of products and services you offer? If not they could be attracted elsewhere if someone new comes along with an answer to a problem you didn't even know about. You could be missing out on new business opportunities with existing customers.

## Your challenge

You will need to introduce a system for reviewing your existing customers' ongoing and changing needs. Your system will need to fit with customers' schedules, your resources and will need to produce feedback that you are able to action in the appropriate way.

## What are the key elements of a successful review?

### The right approach

It is important to use a customer review opportunity to build on your existing relationship. Your customers are busy like you and will need to be given a good reason to spend the time reviewing their needs with you. So your approach is key. Just inviting your customer for a long lunch without setting up the reason for that lunch is likely to waste both your time and theirs. You have to give them a reason to meet you. The review meeting could be set up as a form of regular free consultancy, where you follow a distinct structure looking at the past, present and future.

## The right time

It is a good idea to set up the expectation of this with every new customer. It could become part of your commitment to your customers when you start your relationship. Your review meetings need to be set at a time that anticipates any changing needs your customers might have. This might be annually at the end of their financial year, or end of the year. It might be biannually. It might be seasonally. Each business and customer relationship may differ. The time needs to be right for both parties.

## The right preparation

To successfully review your customers you will need to have full details of their purchasing history with you. You can anticipate some future needs based on past patterns. Taking the time to find out a little about their marketplace and industry may also predict some future needs of which the customer themselves might not yet be aware. You will need to have available a list and/or samples of the work that you have completed for them.

## The right questions

Your review will need an outcome and an action plan both of which can be achieved with the right questions guiding the review. Here is a list of some questions that you might like to incorporate into your customer reviews.

- What do you want to achieve at our review meeting?
- How happy/satisfied have you been with the service/product we have provided for you over $x$ period?
- What, if anything, could we improve on?
- In terms of the services we offer, what is most important to you?
- What are some of the problems you anticipate might need solving in $x$ area over the next year?
- What is your focus for the next six months to a year?
- What are your priorities?
- How could we help you over the next 12 months?

*An action plan and new proposal*

It is important to have an agreed action plan at the end of the review which could be confirmed by a review proposal for future business. A good structure for a review proposal is as follows:

- introduction
- summary of achievements over *x* period
- your feedback
- your aims for *y* period
- suggested solution/proposal/follow up
- price
- next step.

Create yourself a template that you can adapt for use with all your customers. This will save you considerable time and effort.

**YOUR REVIEW – SPECIAL RESPONSE CHECKLIST**
- ▶ Who are you going to review? – make a list.
- ▶ How are you going to approach it? – what is in it for your customers?
- ▶ Decide on a timescale for completing your reviews and set a deadline.
- ▶ What is your aim for each review?
- ▶ How are you going to structure your review? – what questions do you need to ask?
- ▶ Have you done your preparation? – can you anticipate any future demand or needs?
- ▶ What information do you anticipate each customer will want to know about your new products and services? Do you have that information to hand?
- ▶ Have you got a proposal template to use for following up reviews?

## How to use this information

If you do decide to review your existing customers' needs in a structured and focused way, it will be useful to measure the outcome noticing the impact that it has on your business.

> *Think customer review and build*
> *more business for the future*

# 37 Encouraging referrals and recommendations

## What is a referral?

A referral is when one of your satisfied customers who trusts and values what you do, actively refers your service to other potential customers. Having referred you they will give you the potential customer's contact details to follow up. You are in control of the follow up.

## What is a recommendation?

A recommendation is when one of your satisfied customers simply gives your name to one of their contacts endorsing your service. This contact will call you themselves if and when they need your service. The new potential contact is in control of the follow up.

## Why are they important?

They are important because there really is no better way to get new business easily than through a referral or strong recommendation from someone who is already sold on your product or services. If you are active in encouraging referrals and recommendations you could build your business very inexpensively. People love to refer and recommend someone they have received a good service from. You will find that business that comes from a referral or recommendation is a virtual guarantee. The more trust the potential prospect has in the person that refers or recommends, the more likely they are to buy from you, bypassing any initial concerns or scepticism. This will make it much easier and quicker for you to build business.

## Your challenge

Many people don't like to ask for referrals or recommendations although welcome them with open arms when they get them. Many do not have an active procedure for encouraging referrals and recommendations. Your challenge will be to develop a system for encouraging referrals that you feel comfortable using and that motivates your satisfied customers to help you. You will need to remember that when you have performed and delivered a high standard that delights your customer, most will be more than happy to refer you. This is especially true as most people like helping other people. It is up to you to make it as easy as possible for them to do that.

## What gives referrals and recommendations the best chance of leading to business?

Of course there will be a type of referral or recommended business that is ideal for you and there will be some that do not fit with the type of customer you are looking for. When encouraging referrals you will need to be clear about the type of problems you can solve and the type of potential customers that you are looking for. This will enable your referrers to recognise someone who would benefit from the service you offer.

## How to ask for referrals

The key to getting more referrals is to have a strategy for it and plan ahead of time. If you choose to ask someone at the end of their contract with you to make sure they send people your way they will almost undoubtedly say yes. But will anything happen as a result? ... unlikely. Or if they do, the person they mention you to may still not call because they don't know you and it still feels risky.

There are ways of encouraging referrals and recommendations that ensure that you get the best chance of making personal contact with the referred potential client and that your happy customers do actually take action in generating some for you.

### Timing is key when you ask

When you ask for a referral it is usually best when you are discussing the successful results of your work and your client is at their most enthusiastic about you and what you can do. At this stage you might say 'Who else do you know who would benefit from a service like this?' You then take details of this person there and then.

### Plan ahead what you are going to say

You could also try, 'I am really glad that you are happy with the work that we have done for you. Much of our business comes from referrals or recommendations. Do you know of any business associates who are looking for the same kind of results we were able to accomplish for you?'

*Be clear about what you are looking for*

It is much easier for your clients to think about someone when you are very clear about the kind of person, organisation or problem you are able to help with. 'The kinds of people that I am able to help are small business owners who want to make their marketing work. They may be start-ups or existing businesses which need to create a new or fresh identity in the marketplace.'

*Tell customers how to refer people to you*

You need to stay in control here and not just hand over the reins to your prospective referred customer. If you say, 'If you know someone just get them to call me,' this will just leave it up to chance that they will. Instead you could say, 'If you know someone, give me a call first and we can discuss the best way to approach them'. This puts you back in control of the opportunity.

*Direct them to your website*

If you have a good way of capturing the attention of new prospects and an incentive for getting their details, then asking your referrers to direct prospects to your website is a good idea. People are more likely to check out a website before they call you and if yours is good then it will create a positive first impression.

## Reward your customers for their referrals

If you get a good piece of business from a customer referral you could send them a thank you note and a gift in the post. The chances of that person doing it again for you because they feel appreciated are much higher.

You could also consider referral incentives to encourage customers to give you referrals. This may be a discount voucher for future work with you or other incentives that they would value highly.

## How to use this information

Try it out and see what works for you. Measure the return you get. Make sure you always thank people for any referrals you get and reciprocate if you can.

> **Think referral and get FREE marketing**
> **from your satisfied customers**

 ## 38 Publishing case studies

### What is a case study?

A case study is a description of a piece of business you have carried out for one of your customers. It is a success story that acts as a working example of how the work you have undertaken has yielded practical and positive results.

### Why is getting them published of value?

Case studies are powerful because they speak about real results. Getting case studies published can help both you and your clients. You can help to build your clients' profile as well as offering an added bonus for doing business with you. Business people in similar situations with similar desires can be motivated to take action by reading case studies. Case studies make ideas real, tangible and believable.

### Your challenge

Your challenge will be in researching opportunities to get your case studies published ensuring that you get your clients' buy-in to the idea. You may need to enlist your clients' help in writing the case study content.

### What are the key elements of a publishable case study?

- It must have a strong reader interest.
- It is constructed in a way that is easy for others to relate to.
- It is topical and fits in with the publication's/website's agenda.
- It is well written.
- There are some obvious learning points contained within the study.
- Case studies can be integrated into reader interest articles and used as live examples to illustrate the ideas presented. A good example would be an article that I wrote for a number of publications called 'How to create a memorable brand identity' where we used a number of our clients' re-branding projects to illustrate the points.

## The simple structure of a case study article

- Introduction – brief introduction to the client's history and current situation.
- Description of the main problems they were experiencing.
- Their aspirations for the future.
- Brief description of the proposed solution.
- What you did – the steps you took when working with the client.
- The results.

### USING CASE STUDIES – SPECIAL RESPONSE CHECKLIST

- ▶ What case studies do you have currently that would be worth publishing?
- ▶ What context could you create that would gain reader interest?
- ▶ How could your clients help?
- ▶ Where would you like to get them published?
- ▶ Who do you need to contact? – research relevant publications and find out.
- ▶ What contacts do you have that could help you?

## How to use this information

Consider the opportunities that exist for case studies. You can publish them on your own website, other business-related websites that are looking for reader interest information and as part of articles that you write for business publications or magazines. The local press might also be interested if your case study relates to a local business issue.

> **Think case study and promote success**

# 39 Selling up and selling more

## What is selling up?

Selling up is what you do when you increase the value of the sales transaction at the point at which your customer has made a decision to buy. If this takes place at the point of sale it is often known as a 'bump'. The amount the customer spends is literally bumped up by offering something bigger and of greater value. A good example of a bump can be experienced at any McDonald's or Burger King when you are offered a meal deal or a bigger version of what you have originally ordered.

## Additional complementary products

Selling up can simply be offering additional and complementary products at the point of sale. Shoe shops do this when they offer the special shoe cleaners that are required for the shoes you have bought. Some car service garages do it by offering care car products. Hair salons often offer the products that have been used to create the condition and style you are happy with at the end of your appointment. Beauty salons and health spas sell up by offering you the products that have been used by the therapists during your session. Travel companies sell up when they offer holiday insurance and car hire once you have bought a holiday or a flight.

## Upgrade

Selling up can also be introduced during the sales process by offering an upgrade on the particular model or make a customer is interested in. Many electrical retail outlets do this well. If you do this, selling the added value of the upgrade will be important.

## Packaging

Selling up can also be achieved by packaging your products cleverly. This is covered in more detail in the next chapter.

## Why is selling up important?

Selling up is important because it potentially offers you easy access to a big pot of gold. It is so much more costly both in time and resources continually to strive to attract new customers than it is to sell more to a customer who is standing right in front of you.

## Your challenge

Your challenge will be to find ways to sell up and sell more to your customers that adds perceived value. Any 'up sell' must come across as offering more value, not simply asking for more money. Your staff will need to be aware of all the opportunities to sell more and know enough about the products to make up sell suggestions. Staff should all be given 'bump up' suggestions to make at the point of sale and your challenge will be to make sure that they always make those suggestions.

Some people avoid up selling because they don't want to appear pushy or money-grabbing. This is only an attitude of mind. Up selling can be done pleasantly with a positive attitude and a belief that by offering it you are giving your customer the opportunity to gain maximum value. Communicated in this way the customer is more likely to respond positively.

### How to sell up – special response checklist

▶ Make a list of all the possible 'bump ups' you could make with your products and services.

▶ Create a number of questions that your point of sale staff could ask that would prompt the 'bump ups'.

▶ Make a list of all the products and services that naturally link together and could be sold together as package.

▶ Decide which products and services have a natural upgrade.

▶ Try some of these up sell activities for a period of time and measure the results.

## How to use this information

Implement these selling up suggestions as soon as you can. This is one of the easiest ways to increase your sales results.

> **Think sell up and bump up your profits**

# 40 Packaging your products

## What is packaging?

Packaging your products in the context of marketing your business is about grouping your products or services together to enable you to sell more and your customer to gain greater value for money. Examples of how companies package their products are everywhere. Here are some you might recognise.

- An all-inclusive holiday where the customer pays one price and gets flights, accommodation, food, drink and often sports facilities all bundled together in an attractive package.

- A fast food restaurant that offers a 'meal deal', you get the burger of your choice, fries and a drink for a set price.

- A training company that offers a complete programme of modular sessions that link together.

- A coaching company that offers a set number of coaching sessions over a three or six month period.

- Amazon books package their products in a subtle way by offering you both the book you have requested and a second related book.

- A hotel that offers special weekend breaks inclusive of dinner, bed and breakfast.

- Restaurants which offer special set menus to encourage people to dine at quieter times.

Any business can package their products and services together which potentially could have a very positive effect on sales.


## Why is packaging important?

Packaging will enable you to sell more by

- promoting a higher perceived value to your customer
- automatically allowing you to up sell without having to ask for it
- creating the opportunity to work with your customer over a longer time period
- helping to move slow-moving stock by attaching it to more popular new stock.

Packaging can also help you to get stronger initial commitment from your customer. This will give you a greater opportunity to build a relationship and prove your products' or services' value to them.

Packaging can also ensure that your customer buys enough of your service to make a significant impact. A good example of this would be marketing or business consultancy. In these cases the initial groundwork often provides the foundations on which a longer term plan must be built.

## Your challenge

Your challenge is to create a bundle or package that creates value for your customer and makes marketing sense. You will need to work out what naturally links together to create a complete service. Your package will need to be priced correctly and marketed appropriately.

## What makes a successful package?

- It solves a complete problem that a customer has or is likely to have. A good example of this might be a car service centre that appreciates car owners need to prepare their car for the winter. A special winter car care package that covers everything that might end up a problem to customers at an attractive price could be a very desirable proposition as winter approaches.

- It gives the customer choice. If you go to an Indian or Chinese restaurant with a group of friends the menu offers you a choice of different set menus at different prices. If you go to a garage for a car wash you can usually choose between gold, silver and bronze options. People like to have a choice. Successful packages often offer up to three packaged choices, more than that can confuse the customer and make decision-making harder.

- It takes away or limits the potential hassle a customer may have organising all the various elements of a particular purchase. If you are planning a wedding there is a lot to think about: flowers, hair and make up, reception, entertainment, guest accommodation, photographer, transport to and from the venue, attendants and much more. Wedding packages that consider what is most important to the happy couple and group services together accordingly will be successful.

- The package has a high perceived value for the customer even if some of the add-on elements are lower cost to you. The more perceived value the package has, the more irresistible you will be able to make your offer.

**HOW TO CREATE YOUR OWN PACKAGES – SPECIAL RESPONSE CHECKLIST**
- ▶ Decide what you want your packages to achieve for you.
- ▶ Consider what problems your customers have that a package would solve for them.
- ▶ Consider how you could develop a choice of package content and pricing levels that makes your offer simple and attractive.
- ▶ Consider what value your packages offer your customers.
- ▶ Decide what you are going to call your packages.
- ▶ Test your packages with some existing customers and ask for feedback.

## How to use this information

Once you have developed your packages and are clear and confident that they are right for the people you are targeting, you will need to communicate them. This can be done by describing them in your company brochures, sales letters, direct mail, on your website, in your advertising, on posters and in your proposals. Monitor how well they work for you and be prepared to review their content from time to time as customer demand dictates.

> *Think package and sell more*

 41 Creating a newsletter

## What is a newsletter?

A newsletter is something that you produce and distribute to your customers at regular intervals. Newsletters can be distributed by electronic mail or in a traditional hard copy format by post.

## Why are newsletters valuable?

Newsletters are one of the most powerful tools for generating customer traffic and encouraging more sales from existing customers. A newsletter that offers your customers some information that has a high perceived value will maintain an ongoing relationship between you and the people you have been doing business with. This will keep your name in the forefront of their minds until they need your services again. A newsletter can also act as a business stimulator reminding customers of that problem they need solving, or action that they need to take.

Free newsletters that offer useful ideas and information can also act as bait to attract the attention of new customers. Once these potential customers have signed up to your newsletter you will have the opportunity to communicate with them on a continuing basis. Newsletters can be promoted to attract subscribers who ultimately could become customers.

Newsletters enable you to continue to sell your services by offering advice, suggestions, ideas and recommendations.

## Your challenge

Your challenge will be to create a newsletter that is of use to your potential and actual customers, is easy to put together and uses a system of delivery that is inexpensive and efficient. Publishing a hard copy newsletter can be time consuming and costly. Using on online system for sending out an e-newsletter is by far the more attractive option.* Once you have developed your own simple creation and delivery system, sending out a regular e-newsletter couldn't be easier. Your only challenge will be to decide on its name and write the content.

*You can find a list of recommended e-newsletter and auto response systems by going to our resources page at *www.moneymakingmarketingideas.com*

## What makes a newsletter work?

*A name*

This will give it an identity and brand of its own and will become memorable to the recipients. The name needs to convey value to the recipient and ideally be snappy and easy to say and spell.

My newsletter is called 'Money Making Marketing Ideas'.

*Useful reader-orientated content*

Content can be made up of news, answers to questions, ideas, tips, case studies, articles, recommendations and updates: anything that has perceived value that your customers will look forward to receiving.

*Sent regularly*

Everybody receives so much these days via email you should consider sending your newsletter out once a month or bimonthly. Choosing the same day of the week is a good idea. Choose a day of the week when the people you are targeting are most likely to read the newsletter. Sunday evenings can be good for some businesses or for others Friday afternoons. Once your customers get used to receiving your newsletter they will expect it, so you need to make sure that they get their copy as promised without fail.

*The right length*

If it is useful information then people will read it. Most people these days will tell you that they suffer from information overload. So, bearing that in mind, consider how you can make your newsletter both interesting and easy to read. If it passes this test a newsletter that runs to the equivalent of one or two sheets of A4 paper will be perfectly acceptable. You can also have just as much impact with a much shorter newsletter with links that offer customers who are interested an opportunity to explore further.

*Make it personal*

The newsletters I like reading are the ones where the writer talks from the heart and shares a number of personal experiences in the field of my interest. I personally like to sense humour and character in the words I am reading. It depends what you want your newsletter to achieve and the style you have chosen to deliver your content. If you are giving ideas or answers to problems, sharing stories from your personal experience is a very good way of doing this. People often relate better to a story than they do to logical facts. Make your newsletter a reflection of you.

### HOW TO CREATE YOUR OWN NEWSLETTER – SPECIAL RESPONSE CHECKLIST

▶ Decide who you are targeting with your newsletter.

▶ What information would be of value to your readers?

▶ Find out about your customers' interests by running a short survey.

▶ Ask your customers what some of their burning questions are about subjects related to your business. These questions could be answered in your newsletter content.

▶ Look at what else is being written about in newsletters in your industry.

▶ Find out where you could access important information on a regular basis that could be of value to your readers.

▶ Use a standard format to create the layout. Use the same layout, design, colour and structure for every newsletter. This will promote consistency which will help you to build your brand identity and credibility with your audience.

▶ Make sure that you get your newsletter fully proof-read and edited. Silly mistakes can damage your credibility as an expert in your field.

▶ Test your newsletter before you send it out to your complete database. Send it to a colleague or two and ask them to give you feedback.

▶ Make sure that you ask your customers for feedback about the newsletter's value to them. Ask for suggested improvements and do your best to incorporate the ideas you receive.

## How to use this information

The success of your newsletter will be dependent on the number and quality of people that sign up to it. Read the chapters of this book that give you valuable information about building a customer database, opt in email list and driving traffic to your website. This will enable you to create a complete marketing system of which your newsletter will be one important part.

> **Think newsletter and keep your customers interested in you**

# 42 Making the most of email marketing

## What is email marketing?

Almost everyone uses email to communicate these days. Most households have a home computer and an email address even if they are not in business. Many people open their emails before they open their post.

Email marketing is what you do when you use the email system we are all familiar with to promote your business to your customers. This may take the form of a simple straightforward email or email newsletter. There are several very good services on the market today that enable you to build email lists easily through website marketing activities and communicate via bulk email as often as you want or need to.

Email marketing can be used for appointment reminders, special offers, useful information or ideas, new product launches, new services, competitions and more.

## Why is email marketing valuable?

Email marketing is an excellent low cost way of keeping in regular contact with both existing and potential customers. The people you come into contact with during the course of your marketing and networking activities may not all be ready to do business with you right now. If, however, you give them a very good reason to provide you with their email address and permission to keep in touch, the chances of you being around when they are ready to buy are much higher.

Email marketing is easy and quick to do and you can potentially communicate with large numbers of people in a very personal way. Email marketing is potentially much more valuable to you than a costly direct mail campaign.

## Your challenge

You will need to consider the amount of spam that the majority of people get bothered by on a daily basis. It can be overwhelming for many people. Your email needs to be something that people welcome. You will need to think very carefully about what you use it for. Email marketing may be quick but it is not something that should be put together in a hurry. You will need to create a situation where people look forward to your email because they think that they are going to get something of value from it. You also need to be careful not to overdo it. Sending emails every day or even every week can be just too much for many people. You will need to gauge what is right for your client base and be sensitive to their needs.

When you use email marketing your email address is a major part of your marketing message, so it is important to get this right. It will need to be easy to use and easy to remember. If it is long-winded with lots of letters and words that are difficult to spell the chances are that you will lose some business because of it. Your email should read in a way which helps you come across as credible business.

So choose email addresses that make it completely clear what business you are in and make them as easy and as straight-forward as you can to use.

## What makes email marketing work?

To make this work you will need to build a good list of prospects first. This is covered in Chapter 16 in the section on how to build an opt-in mailing list.

### HOW TO CREATE YOUR OWN EMAIL MARKETING SYSTEM – SPECIAL RESPONSE CHECKLIST

▶ Do you think that email marketing could work for you?

▶ How are you going to attract email addresses and get permission to communicate?

▶ You will need to investigate the internet based email marketing systems that are available.* You may consider auto response systems that can be set up to run sequences of emails.

▶ Make sure you have a system for recording the email addresses that you collect. A spreadsheet is a simple way of doing this. This can be uploaded into your email contact database or any online system that you use.

▶ You will need to create your email campaign ideas and decide how you can keep your prospects interested in you and your business. Remember to focus on giving something of value, as opposed to solely pitching your services.

▶ Make sure that you get your emails proof-read. Sending out bulk emails with spelling or grammatical errors is not good for your professional image.

▶ Send out a test email to yourself and another person and look at it from the customers' point of view before you press the button on the complete database.

▶ Consider how you will measure and monitor the response you get.

*You will find those I recommend by going to our website *www.moneymakingmarketingideas.com* and exploring the resources section.

## *How to use this information*

Email marketing can work very well for you if you take time to set up a system to attract and deliver efficiently. If you have experienced junk mail you will know what annoys you and clogs up the inbox. You must avoid doing this at all costs. If you use email marketing it must be targeted and valuable. Concentrate on this and you will be successful.

> **Think email marketing and communicate cheaply and easily**

# 43 Using hospitality and special days

You can build stronger relationships with both your key customers and prospective clients by inviting them to join you for hospitality at special events. Corporate hospitality is available at a variety of memorable and important events both at home and overseas. A day at the races, a box at the British Grand Prix, a party at the Henley Royal Regatta, tickets for Wimbledon or world cup football are just some of the things you can do. You can provide a special tent or table dedicated to your organisation and the pleasure of your guests. You can organise this yourself or you can use the services of any number of corporate hospitality and event organisers.

You can offer your clients opportunities to find out more about your products and services by creating special events that educate them and provide fun and entertainment at the same time. There is a section in Chapter 11 of this book that focuses solely on how to use events and talks to sell your business.

You can invite clients and their teams to join you and your teams for a day of fun and bonding by going go-carting, playing golf, sailing or partying at a polo match.

You can take your clients out for a special lunch or dinner or to the theatre. You can invite them to special conferences or congresses abroad. Christmas parties or summer barbeques can be a less expensive way of providing fun and entertainment if you have a smaller budget.

## Why are invitations to special events important?

Being invited to a unique special event or day out can be exciting for your customers. It will make them feel highly valued by you. The invitation acknowledges their importance to you. This can only be good for your relationship with them. If the event you choose is high profile you stand to gain the kudos that goes with it. People will want to attend the event and will connect your organisation with giving them that opportunity. If you simply go out and have fun with your customers and get to know them in a social setting, you will create the opportunity to build a much stronger connection. People do business with people who they like and trust. This is one of the greatest rapport-building opportunities.

## *Your challenge*

Your challenge will be to choose the right events and not to spend your entire marketing budget in one go. Providing corporate hospitality and tickets for high profile events can be expensive so you need to weigh up the potential the event has for building stronger existing client relationships and introducing new ones.

If you do decide to have a hospitality tent, room or table at an event you will need to make sure that you make the most of it. This will take planning and organising.

## *What makes hospitality and special days work?*

- You must be clear exactly what you want the event to achieve for you.
- Choose the right event and the right mix of people.
- Make sure it is well organised from invitation to follow up.
- Staff are fully briefed, each having an important role to play.
- The senior people in your organisation commit to attend the day.
- Your guests' names are remembered.
- The day is used to reinforce your organisation's values.
- You look after your guests and put their well-being and enjoyment at the top of your priority list.
- If you offer your guests the opportunity to find out more about the people in your organisation, take the time to find out more about them too.
- Consider creative ways to help your guests relax and get to know each other.
- It should be more social than business – it is nice just to relax sometimes.
- Make sure that you have a proper follow-up system in place.
- Get feedback – find out what your guests think about the day.

**HOSPITALITY EVENT OR SPECIAL DAY – SPECIAL RESPONSE CHECKLIST**
- ▶ What do you want the day to achieve? (customer/team bonding, new business, keep existing customers, product launch, say thank you).
- ▶ Who would you invite and why?
- ▶ What are the interests of the people you are considering?
- ▶ What events do you think your guests would connect with?
- ▶ Which events would give your organisation some distinction?
- ▶ What needs planning? (invitations, hospitality area layout and design, seating plans, time-table, team briefing, follow up).
- ▶ How will you measure the success of the event?
- ▶ How will you know personally if it has been successful?

## How to use this information

If you haven't considered using hospitality, special days out or events to build your client relationships maybe this is your chance to do that. Investigate what you could do. Ask your clients what they would like to do and get your best ones involved in your decision making process. Ask your team what they think. Try it and see what happens.

> **Think hospitality and have some fun with your clients**

# 11

# Marketing methods that attract new customers

**inspiring ways
to market
your small business**

# 44 Building host relationships

## *What is a host relationship?*

Host beneficiary relationships are based on harnessing the existing goodwill and strong relationships that all sorts of other businesses have already established with prime prospects for your own product or service. If you form a relationship with a business that is not in direct competition with you but sells to the same people as you, potentially you could both help each other.

> **Examples of this might be:**
> A conservatory company might form a host relationship with a building company or an estate agent.
>
> A business consultant might form a host relationship with an accountant or a solicitor.
>
> A plumber might form a host relationship with an electrician.
>
> A print, copy and design company may form a host relationship with a website company or a marketing company.

A business you might form a host relationship with will tend to be selling something that goes before, goes along with or follows the product or service you would sell to these people.

## *Why are host relationships valuable?*

Forming host relationships is a very easy way to get access to potential new customers who could be in the market for your products and services. Because your host already has a relationship with their customers they can provide a solid and trusted foundation for you to start from. If a host is willing to recommend your services to their customers it provides you with free marketing.

## *Your challenge*

Your challenge is to open your mind to all the possible relationships you could form and be creative in your thinking. Ask yourself who in your business area already sells to the customers you want to reach or serve. Make a list. Now think about why someone should offer you a host. To develop strong host relationships you will need to sell yourself and your service in a way that makes it attractive. Hosts are only going to agree to recommend your services when they feel confident that you will deliver to a high standard.

## What makes a host relationship successful?

A host relationship works best when there is no competition and both services naturally complement each other. If by recommending your service your host adds value to their own customer relationship it will have served two important purposes.

> **A good host relationship is a relationship of trust and rapport**

**HOW TO SET UP HOST RELATIONSHIPS – SPECIAL RESPONSE CHECKLIST**

▶ Make a list of all the things your customers might buy that are associated with the reason they use your services. For example if you sell insurance what might your customers have bought beforehand that would prompt the need for the insurance – car, house, a business? A coffee distribution company which deals with the catering industry might add food or other beverage suppliers to their list.

▶ Make a list of all the contacts you already have with people who provide some of the services associated with your own. Consider how you could build a host relationship with these businesses.

▶ What could you offer that would give them a chance to experience your service themselves? Once they have tested you out themselves, with a good experience behind them, they are more likely to have confidence in you. You could offer a 'free' experience of your service for a period of time to enable the evaluation of its potential value to their customers. You could also offer a selection of customer testimonials.

▶ Choose a selection to make contact with. You could call, email or write in the first instance.

▶ Set up meetings that allow you to explore the best way of working together.

▶ Discuss ways in which your service could add value to their existing customer service.

▶ Ask what they would need to know about your service to feel confident enough to recommend you.

▶ Provide what they need to start the process and agree a periodic review for feedback.

**Sample letter/email to open the door to a host relationship**

Dear

I noticed that you currently offer $x$ service to $y$ people. We are a business that offers $z$ service to a similar customer base. As we are not in direct competition with each other, but offer services that potentially complement and support each other, I wondered if you might be interested in discussing a way in which we could recommend each others' services to our mutual advantage. I will give you a call during this next week to arrange to have a conversation at your convenience if this suggestion sounds worth exploring further.

Kind regards

## How to make the most of your host relationships

There are many ways in which you could work your host relationships to mutual advantage. One way might be that your host agrees to give your card and a verbal recommendation each time they see an opportunity with one of their customers. Or they may agree to include a recommendation in their e newsletter. You may swap website links. You may get included in their pre or post-sales communication.

You may develop a financial incentive to encourage your host to look out for opportunities to pass business your way, or you may simply agree to help each other without financial recompense. Either way your arrangements need to suit both parties and be ultimately orientated to make it easy and attractive for customers to buy.

> **Think host and reach more customers easily**

# 45 Using joint ventures

## What is a joint venture?

A joint venture is when you are given permission to use other people's customers to get new business. Joint venture marketing is the process of marketing to customers of complementary businesses. Joint venture means that you get the cooperation of the businesses that acquired the customers in the first place and that the relationships you create with your partners is win-win. The relationship you set up might involve your joint partner endorsing your product or service through their own customer database in return for the same or an agreed commission on sales made. This can also be known as affiliate marketing. Many web-based businesses use this method to increase sales.

> **Examples**
>
> An interior design company could potentially share customers with landscape gardeners, builders, bedroom furniture companies, antiques, bathroom and kitchen companies.
>
> A hair salon could share customers with a gym, a beauty salon, a nail bar or nutritional therapist.
>
> A hotel with restaurants, bars, tourist attractions or the theatre.

Joint venture marketing can be carried out by email, direct mail, sales letter or newsletter.

## Why are joint ventures valuable to you?

Many businesses share common customers. These common customers all have the potential to spend money on related products and services. With so much choice available to customers, any short-cuts to a reliable and trusted supplier endorsed by someone you already do business with will be appreciated.

Joint venture marketing is your short cut to getting your product or service in front of more people in a fraction of the time it would take you to create the same customer list yourself. By using joint partners you will end up marketing to a very warm and highly targeted market.

## *Your challenge*

Your challenge will be to open your mind to all the possible complementary joint partners available to you, then find and educate them to the potential benefits of joint ventures. You will need to understand their interests, possible objections and be able to offer an incentive that is attractive enough to motivate them to take part.

## *What makes a joint venture successful?*

- When it is win-win and both parties are comfortable and trust the arrangements.

- When it is properly planned and professionally implemented.

- When you can give your joint partner a simple method of letting their customers know about your products and services. Provide a sales letter or copy for an email as this will make it easy for your joint partner. The easier it is, the more likely they are to do it.

- When you can let your joint partners know how much business their list generated and reward them for it.

- When it is risk-free for the joint venture partner.

- When you offer something to the joint partner or your joint partner's customers that is perceived as valuable. Some joint partners will see that being able to offer their customers something extra, getting them a free consultation or a discounted introduction will rub off on their own business relationship.

### HOW TO SET UP JOINT VENTURES – SPECIAL RESPONSE CHECKLIST
- ▶ Think about how this could potentially work for your business.
- ▶ Make a list of potential complementary or related products or services.
- ▶ Make a list of all the businesses that sell those products and services in your target geographical areas.
- ▶ Get the names of the business owners.
- ▶ Send a letter introducing yourself outlining your idea and proposing a meeting to explore further. You can ask in your letter whether they could be interested in making extra money with no extra effort.
- ▶ Make a follow-up call to set up the appointment.
- ▶ At the meeting explore their interests and discuss a win-win case for a joint venture.

## *How to use this information*

Joint ventures are an excellent way for small business owners to leverage the goodwill each has established with their individual customer bases. Open your mind and make the most of the opportunities that exist for this. It may not be something that you have ever thought of doing before. Try it out.

> **Think joint venture and double up on your customer contact**

# 46 Working 'word of mouth'

## What is word of mouth?

Word of mouth is what happens when people tell people about you. Word of mouth is happening when potential customers hear about your service on the grapevine. They may hear about you from someone who has never even used your service.

Word of mouth is a way of getting business when people talk positively about you and your service. These people may be satisfied customers of yours or they may be people who have simply heard about others' satisfaction with your product or service.

Word of mouth advertising happens when you get known through the conversations people have with each other. This may result in referrals or recommendation. Many people get most or all of their new business through word of mouth advertising.

I had a conversation recently with a friend who wants to plan her financial future and needed some advice. She asked if I knew anybody she could talk to. I gave two people a very good word of mouth advert.

## Why is it important?

Word of mouth is *free*. It is important because as it builds up over time it can provide you with an ongoing supply of new business without you having to do anything at all.

## Your challenge

Word travels fast when you do something extraordinarily good for someone. It also travels just as fast when something goes wrong and the customer complains. Your challenge will be to continually provide a level of service high enough to 'wow' your existing customers and build a level of trust and rapport that prompts those who use you both to remember and recommend you to others.

## What makes word of mouth successful?

- When people feel motivated to talk about you to others.
- When they like and trust you and the work you do.
- When you have done a really good job for someone.
- When you provide an extra special service or go the extra mile.
- When you provide your customers with leads or referrals.
- When you keep in touch with those you have done business with, ensuring that they remember the experience they had.
- When you make a connection with the people you do business with and they really feel that you care.

## How to get word of mouth working for you

### Be the best

All you really have to do is concentrate on doing the absolute best you can for the customers you have. You need to put into practice all of the profile building and communication techniques outlined in later chapters of this book. To make word of mouth work you need to be worth talking about and you must be memorable both as a person and as a business.

The longer you have been in business providing an excellent service, the more likely it is that word of mouth advertising will be working for you.

### Promote your success stories

If you are a new business you can encourage word of mouth by promoting the success stories you have. Publishing customers' testimonials in your marketing materials can help to build conviction in your offering. By talking about the problems you have solved for your customers and the results they have achieved you give potential customers a chance to recognise themselves or the people they know.

When that happens you are more likely to get word of mouth business.

### Show appreciation

When you get a piece of word of mouth business you can encourage more by showing appreciation for it. A gift, thank you or invitation to one of your special social events will reinforce the goodwill you have created and motivate more.

*Reciprocation increases momentum*

Show what word of mouth means to you by reciprocating the gesture. Spread the word about your customers' businesses and you will see the word of mouth momentum increasing.

**IS WORD OF MOUTH WORKING AS WELL AS IT CAN FOR YOU? – SPECIAL RESPONSE CHECKLIST**

▶ How much word of mouth business do you get?

▶ How do you measure word of mouth business?

▶ How do you say thank you and encourage more from the people who have generated it for you?

▶ What could you do to promote your success stories and spread the word?

▶ What could you do to accelerate your word of mouth advertising?

## How to use this information

Word of mouth is the best natural form of advertising there is. Focus your attention on what you can do to stimulate its impact on your business and you will see your business grow.

> **Think word of mouth and increase the talk-talk about you**

# 47 Educating customers

## What is customer education?

Customer education is all about giving your customers an opportunity to learn more about your products or services. The more people understand about the value they could receive, the more likely they are to buy. The degree to which a potential customer needs to appreciate the context within which the product or service they are purchasing exists will vary. Offering customer education can be a very good way of getting those potential customers to put their hands up and say 'I'm interested in what you have to offer'. For some businesses, education can be the first step in the sales process. Many buyers spend some time researching for information before they are ready to choose a supplier.

## Why is it important?

People may willingly pay more for most products or services as long as they understand and appreciate the value they're receiving. Not knowing, not being aware or not understanding can slow up the buying process.

Sometimes an idea or information provided by a business can stimulate a desire to buy.

Many of your potential clients certainly do not know as much about your service as you do and it may be that they don't fully understand and appreciate

- how it could benefit them
- how it works
- the opportunities that exist
- how you can help avoid problems
- how to maximise the benefits once they have used your service
- the full level of service they can expect from you.

The more people understand and appreciate how a product or service can benefit or improve their life or their business, the more they'll want it and the more closely connected they'll become to you if you help them to find this out.

## *Your challenge*

Your challenge will be to make yourself aware of what a customer needs to know. You will also need to choose the best and most effective method of delivering that information.

## *How can you educate your customers?*

There are a number of ways in which you can do this:

- Write articles
- Give demonstrations
- Run talks
- Offer training or awareness days
- Offer samples
- Write a book
- Free consultations
- Frequently asked questions on your website or brochure
- Information CD
- Tele seminars or teleconferences
- Online demonstrations or presentations
- Exhibitions

If your customer education is presented in a relevant and interesting way it will attract more people.

**Real life examples**

A company providing online human resource software runs teleconferences and consultant development days. These are both free services and are designed to provide enough business stimulation and ideas to generate a desire to use the software.

One of our most successful customer education projects has been running a series of talks and writing a number of articles featuring appropriate case studies. One very popular talk was entitled 'How to create a memorable brand,' as well as offering a fun and educational evening for potential customers, also stimulated an interest in our branding service.

A solar energy company who wished to convert customers who used conventional home heating services to solar power recognised that education would be a vital element in the sales process, as the benefits of solar power are largely unknown. One of the methods chosen to do this was a mobile showroom along with some well presented information on their website.

Many property and financial investment companies use educational seminars as a first step in their sales process.

### CUSTOMER EDUCATION – SPECIAL RESPONSE CHECKLIST

▶ How do you currently educate your customers?
▶ What don't your customers know about you?
▶ What do you think they need to know in order to buy?
▶ Find out from your customers by asking what questions they have.
▶ Consider the best way to deliver that information to them.
▶ Be creative in your approaches.
▶ Consider how much detail they need.
▶ Monitor how well whatever you choose to do works.
▶ When you provide education, create a system that allows you to capture customers' details. Keep a record of that customer information.
▶ Make sure that you create a follow up continued education process.

## How to use this information

Use this information to make a plan to improve the education of your customers. You may find more ideas about how you can do this as you read the sections on newsletters, events, conferences, article writing and exhibiting at conferences.

> **Think educate and attract those hungry for knowledge and ideas**

# 48 Using events and talks to sell your business

## What are talks and events?

A talk is when you speak about a subject of interest to your target audience at either your own or a host's event. An event is an occasion that either you or a host creates to connect with target customers and offer an opportunity to build relationships and for those customers to learn more about your products and services in the process. Some examples of an event might be speed networking, a conference, a party, wine tasting, an exhibition, dinner with a guest speaker, a debate, a teleconference or a demonstration.

## Why are they important?

Special events can give you great distinction and connection with your customers and they can be a lot of fun! You offer your prospects or customers a chance to come to you to learn and be stimulated.

A special event gives you the opportunity to attract potential customers through giving them something of value. This needs to be something that ultimately connects with you and your product or service. You could share some up-to-date research data, provoke a discussion, demonstrate a product or service. If this is run well, it will provoke interest in you and your service without you having to sell it.

## Your challenge

Getting people to attend your event will be your biggest challenge. They will only come if they can see clearly what is in it for them. You need to do your research and find out what people ultimately could be interested in. What are the current hot topics, what are the major problems your target customer group faces? When would they be most likely to come – is a breakfast or evening event better? What about trying out some new technology and using teleconference facilities – that way your audience reach is likely to be wider.

## What makes an event or talk successful?

■ The right target people attend.

- They enjoy it and get personal value out of it.
- You get positive feedback.
- Attendees want to make contact with you for business as a direct consequence of the impact the event or talk had on then.
- You are in a position to follow up the leads generated by the event.
- You generate a positive return on your investment of time and resource.

### WHAT TO CONSIDER WHEN PLANNING AN EVENT OR TALK – SPECIAL RESPONSE CHECKLIST
*Events*

▶ What have you done in the past that has worked?

▶ What have you yourself attended that has been good?

▶ How could you use an event to promote your services?

▶ Who currently runs events that attract the kind of audience you want to reach?

▶ What would your target audience be interested in?

▶ The timing – when, where and how long? Make sure that it doesn't clash with public or school holidays. Consider when your target audience are most likely to want to attend that event. Bad timing can put people off.

*Talks*

▶ What could you talk about that might ultimately result in some interest in an element of your business?

▶ Research your initial ideas with your target audience and the people who are in regular contact with them.

▶ The title of the talk – will it attract the attention of your audience?

▶ Your description of the potential value the talk offers.

### HOW TO CREATE OPPORTUNITIES FOR TALKS – SPECIAL RESPONSE CHECKLIST

▶ Networking events – are there any networking events that your target customer attends on a regular basis that you could talk at?

▶ Breakfast meetings – are there any business groups that meet throughout the month?

▶ Chamber of commerce – could you speak at one of their events?

▶ Round table.

▶ Conferences or trade shows.

▶ Business shows.

▶ Could you run your own event in association with Business Link who offer free event marketing in return for an opportunity to promote Business Link at your event?

**Sample event feedback card**

Thank you for attending this event.

To help us to improve what we do we would appreciate your feedback.

**Name**................................................................................

**Address** ...........................................................................

**Telephone**.........................................................................

**Mobile** .............................................................................

**Email**................................................................................

What did you find of most value? ........................................

What did you find of least value?.........................................

What action do you plan to take as a result of attending this event/talk? ...................

................................................................................................

What else would interest you if we were to run a similar event in the future?...............

................................................................................................

**I am interested in (tick box)**

Receiving free newsletter            ☐

Receiving free report                    ☐

Receiving free consultation          ☐

Further information about.....................................................

☐  Please tick this box if you do not want to receive our regular information alerts

**Thank you for your help**

## How to make the most of your talks and events

To make the most of your talk or event – whether you run it yourself or speak at a host's event – you will need to make sure that you get the attendees' contact details for follow-through marketing. An event feedback card is not only a useful way for you to measure what was appreciated by your attendees, but also gives an opportunity to ask for opt-in to the next step. That step might be agreement to receive ongoing information and ideas from your organisation which might be to have a free consultation or receive a free report. If you can offer something at the event that encourages attendees to take the next step in your sales process it will make it much easier for you to convert.

> *Think talk and help your customers get*
> *the answers to their burning questions*

# 49 Driving business to your website

If you are about to get a website designed the first question and most important question you need to answer is...

## What do you want your website to achieve for you?

Maybe you want to use your site

- as an online brochure
- to create a professional and credible image
- to sell products directly
- to take orders
- to attract new potential customers to contact you for information
- to provide information
- to generate the email addresses of subscribers to your newsletters and free reports.

Whatever it is that you want to achieve, it will require you to drive traffic to your site to get it.

## How to drive traffic to your site

*Tell your customers about your website*

Publish your website on everything that you use to promote your business. Your business card, your brochure, your sales letters, your compliment slips, your company magazines, your invoices, your advertising, your vehicle livery, as part of your window display. It is useful if the website name is both easy to remember and contains keywords in its title.

*Give your customers a good reason to go to your website*

Give your customers a good reason to go to your website. Invite them there by offering something of value when they get there.

- An article.
- Free information.
- Book a free consultation.
- A free trial or test.

- An online demonstration or presentation.
- A competition linked to information on your website.

Promote these incentives in your daily communication with existing and potential customers.

## Increase your link popularity

Link popularity is the total number of websites that link to your site. Good quality link popularity can dramatically increase traffic to your website. Well placed links are an excellent source of consistent and targeted traffic. They can also even generate additional search engine traffic to your site.

Increasing the number of quality relevant sites which link to your site can actually improve your search engine rankings.

### What is a good quality link?

A good quality link is another organisation that already has achieved search engine popularity and is relevant to your business. A link is when your website address appears on another business site. They can be achieved in a number of ways.

- Joining online directories for your specific industry niche.
- Joining networking directories.
- Banner advertising on relevant sites.
- Article writing for other sites.
- Reciprocal links with partners and host relationships.
- Banner advertising.

### How do you know who to link to?

The trick is to run a test search and find your most popular competitors. Go to *www.linkpopularity.com* and type their details into the free search box. You can find out how many links they have and who those links are. This will give you a head start. Research all the links they have and choose the ones that you think will work for you. You can also use this tool to find out who is linked to your site already. It will allow you to research Google, Yahoo! and MSN.

## *Improve your search engine ranking*

Search engine optimisation means making the most of your website content to enable you to rank highly in search engines. The higher your rank the more likely people are to find you when they search for the products or services you offer.

This is a highly skilled and time consuming process which is why many companies recruit a specialist website marketer to work with them over time to build up and fine tune their approach.

### *How do the search engines rank your website?*

It depends on a number of factors.

■ How many sites link to yours.
■ How many pages your site has.
■ The words in your website name.
■ Keywords.
■ Words in bold.
■ Words in URL.
■ Having more than 300 words on your home page.
■ Keyword density.
■ Google page ranking.

If you are prepared to go through a steep learning curve there are things that you can do yourself.

### *Find out what your keywords are*

Keywords are the terms and phrases you would naturally associate with whatever you sell. Ask yourself if you were searching for your products and services using a search engine what would you type in the box.

Brainstorm all the words that you think a prospective customer/visitor would enter into the search engines. Ask your customers, friends and family what they would enter. You can put yourself into the position of someone searching for your product and service. How do they think and what would they be most likely to put into a search engine?

The **Overture search assistant** tool is one of the most useful resources I have found for exploring how many searches in the last month were made on particular key words. Here is the link for this *free* tool and some basic steps to take: *www.overture.com*

- Choose your country.
- Go to the basics of search marketing.
- Go to right tool for the job.
- Click on to keywords which will take you to the keyword assistant. You can type in all the keyword combinations on your list and find out how many times they were searched for in the last month.
- Look out for the search term suggestion tool.

You can also:

- include your keywords in your website title
- include your keywords in your copy
- repeat in different ways on each page on your site.

## Google search for your competition

You can also type your keywords into the Google search engine and see what comes up. This will be your competition. Look at the top right hand corner of the screen and see what the results are for the number of sites that come up with that particular keyword combination.

The best keywords to use are the ones that have the best website to search ratio. This means the keywords with the highest number of searches (found through overture) and the least number of websites using that combination. The better your website : search ratio the less competition there is for you to beat.

## Article publishing

Did you realise that thousands of business owners use a simple technique to generate targeted visitors to their websites without paying a pound in advertising?

*How is it done?*

By creating tightly focused articles other people publish in their ezines (online magazines and email newsletters) and post on their websites. This method rates so powerfully that some even call it 'the web's best kept traffic secret'.

Now, you may ask, 'Why would an ezine publisher or website owner publish my articles for their subscribers?' The answer: content!

Over a 100,000 ezines and e-newsletters operate on the web (along with millions of websites) covering everything from pets and cooking to investments and property. Many of them need tightly focused content and they simply can't produce all of it themselves.

You can get valuable publicity, exposure you often couldn't even pay for if you wanted to, by providing valuable, content-rich articles in exchange for a byline and a link to your website.

## Pay per click

Pay per click advertising simply means paying to put an advert for your website at or near the top of the search engines. When you search for something on Google or Yahoo! you may have read the term 'sponsored listings' that is pay per click advertising. You are paying to get to the top of the search engines. It is called pay per click because you only pay when someone clicks on the link to visit your site. The site that comes out top of the search engines will be the one which has bid the highest amount per click. You have to put in a bid for the top position. To set this up for yourself you will have to sign up for a pay per click account for the search engines that you wish to advertise in. You can take a look at the top sites in the sponsored listing for the search term you would like to use and see what their current bids are. If the top site bid was £1.40 per click you would have to bid more than that to take the number one spot. It is the same for each level. To generate a good level of traffic to your site it is best to be on the first page.

It is up to you how much you want to spend per day and you can set your own budget. You can set a maximum daily budget and when that budget is exceeded you would drop out of the rankings until the next day. That will make sure that you only spend what you are comfortable spending each day to get the clicks to your site.

There are online tutorials that explain step by step how to achieve your pay per click programme. Google and Overture are the main search engines that sell pay per click.

## Email and e-newsletter campaigns

Email and newsletter campaigns are another great way to drive traffic to your site. A direct link to your site can be used which makes it easy for readers to click through immediately. You will need to provide a good reason for the customers you are targeting to click through to your site. You need to provide something of value to your customers that can only be retrieved by accessing your site.

## When you get traffic keep them there!

Ninety-nine people out of 100 when surfing the web will visit sites and leave within eight seconds unless the site gives them a very good reason to stay. So when you get traffic to your site you need to make sure that the site is attractive enough to your visitors.

The best websites are the ones that have clear, obvious navigation buttons, an attractive professional image, are visually appealing, communicate instantly what is being sold, are easy to read and give you all the information you need at the click of a button. Websites that use all the bells and whistles are not usually the best selling sites.

## How to use this information

Implementing and fine tuning strategies for driving traffic to your website is an ongoing task. You may find that now you understand the basics of what is involved and can see the potential you may decide to utilise the services of those that specialise in website marketing. Alternatively you may have someone in your business with the aptitude for creating and implementing your own internal website marketing plan.

> **Think website traffic and drive sales up**

# 50 Networking for the right reasons

## What is networking?

Networking is all about developing business contacts and relationships that enable you to expand your business base. It is also about increasing your knowledge and building your profile in the community.

The purpose of networking is to make connections with people and build new relationships and trust.

Networking is a two way process. It is about giving as well as getting. As you meet new people and build up your contacts you may find yourself able to refer or recommend people or use their services yourself.

Networking can be a longer term strategy for building new business. You may not see a return from it for months or years. It can also be immediate. My own personal experience of networking has been very positive and I have found myself making at least one very worth-while business relationship at every networking event I have attended.

Networking is a great way to meet new people. There are so many different types of networking events to choose from. If you are an early riser, a breakfast meeting might suit, or an evening event if you prefer. There are speed networking events, profit clubs, lunches, boat trips, theatre visits, trade shows, conferences, presentations, speaker sessions, discussion groups and more.

The most important thing is to choose the networking event, locations and target audience that most suits what you are looking for.

## Why is it important?

If you work alone, attending a regular networking event can ensure that you continue to get out and about and mix with people. This is important. Meeting and communicating with people is a vital part of business building, and keeping up the habit will make the task easier. If worked correctly, networking is an excellent way of generating more leads and clients for your business.

## Your challenge

To be a valuable marketing method, networking needs to be practised in the correct way otherwise it can be a complete waste of time. You will need to make sure that you attend the events that give you the best chance of meeting people who fit with your ideal customer profile. You will also need a method of ensuring that you both meet and follow through on any potential new relationship.

If you find it hard to walk into a group situation and communicate with new people, you could initially find the nature of networking challenging. Networking lunches, educational or sporting events can be good places to start as generally they create a more relaxed social environment with something enjoyable for you to share.

## How to get the most out of networking

- Focus on relationship building not selling.

- Be clear what your own networking goals are.

- Do your research and pick the right events.

- Remember that everyone there is open to talking as they are all there for the same reason.

- Find out about people by asking questions – resist the temptation to simply talk about yourself and your business.

- Listen for some problems or needs that you might be able to help with.

- Speak to as many people as you can – mix and mingle.

- Concentrate on building rapport not selling.

- Enjoy yourself and relax.

- Take some business cards with you (I know this is obvious but some people don't).

- Follow up the people you meet with a brief email or letter.

- If you meet someone you think you could work with set up a meeting to talk in further detail.

- If you get a chance to speak for a few minutes about who you are and what you do, know your USPs and have a short statement that you can make that gets that across and keeps it in people's minds.

- Have an elevator speech that you feel comfortable with – be able to speak easily about how your business helps people and solves problems.

- Be clear about what you are looking for in terms of new business. If you are presenting what you do at a profit or referral club you will get the opportunity to explain what kind of customers you are looking for.

- Build up a few events that you like and go on a regular basis for a while – this will make it easier to build stronger relationships and trust.

- Review your success. How many new contacts made at networking events have ultimately led to more business? Which have proved to be the best events?

- You may need to try and test a number of different events before you hit on exactly the right formula for you.

**MAKING NETWORKING WORK FOR YOU – SPECIAL RESPONSE CHECKLIST**
- ▶ What do you want to achieve through networking?
- ▶ Which networking events could you try that fulfil your criteria?
- ▶ What do you need to prepare in order to get the most out of networking?
- ▶ What is your budget for networking events?
- ▶ How will you measure the success of your networking?

## How to use this information

Get out there and get started. What are you waiting for?

> **Think networking and connect with people**

 # 51 Telemarketing for leads

## *What is telemarketing?*

Telemarketing is a term given to any form of telephone communication with customers that is designed to generate new business.

Telemarketing can be used to:

- follow through on any sales campaign
- follow up on leads generated at networking events or conferences
- follow up leads or contacts made at talks
- survey or research your market and identify potential prospects
- build and progress relationships
- follow up sales letters sent to your customers and prospects providing a likely 20%–50% increase in sales and results
- make preferred offers on your products and services to your best customers
- research or test new ideas.

Telemarketing is anything that is done on the telephone to communicate with existing and potential prospects to generate or progress sales leads.

## *Why is it important?*

Telemarketing is the most direct way of communicating with your potential prospects. Providing you are able to get through to the decision maker you will have an opportunity there and then to move your business marketing forward.

There are some fascinating statistics on telemarketing follow-up calls: 92% of people will have given up after four negative responses, and only 8% of people ask for the order a fifth time. Yet Market Research studies show that 80% of all significant sales result from people who followed up at least five different times after the initial sales contact, before getting a positive response. When you consider that 80% of customers say 'no' four times before they say 'yes', the inference is that 8% of people are getting 80% of the sales!

Consider how long it takes to convert a completely cold prospect for your product or service. How many follow up calls does it take before you finally get the deal or even the first appointment? If you had not followed up religiously would you have been successful? Probably not. So, disciplined telephone follow-up is not just important, it is vital.

We are all busy and your customers are no different. They may well be very interested in a lot of the offers and propositions you have made but they get diverted. They lose things. They forget to respond. They don't get around to acting on it.

You actually do them a fabulous service if you or someone in your business picks up the phone and follows up. The call doesn't have to be pushy; it just needs to be respectfully timed, with the outcome of re-alerting or informing.

If the person who makes these calls always asks if it is convenient to talk and reminds the customer of the last contact with them you cannot fail to increase your chances of doing business with this customer.

It's exciting to know that telephone follow-up can increase the effectiveness of any letter or email contact you send out by up to twenty times.

## Your challenge

Telemarketing takes time, the right person to do it, focus and discipline. If you are going to make this part of your marketing strategy you will need to plan it well. It may be that you need someone in your business specifically focused on this one job. It is pointless to make this a haphazard activity. Details of all the calls made and outcome of those calls will need to be recorded religiously. A good customer contact system is vital. Your challenge will be to set up the system, operate it and measure the return on your investment.

## What makes telemarketing successful?

- When it is delivered in a non-scripted manner, with a clear outcome and confident approach.

- Treat each person and each call as if it was the first.

- Understand the person you have called may be in the middle of something, driving or just about to go into a meeting. Always ask if it is convenient to speak.

- Introduce yourself and explain the purpose of the call.

- Have something to say that is likely to grab the person's attention and make it worth giving you some time.

- If you are using the telephone to make direct contact with prospective clients make sure you qualify the person against your own prospect criteria.

- Follow up.

- As you probably have already experienced, there is usually a right time for your prospects to buy and you need to find out exactly when that is and make sure that your follow-up coincides with that.

- Keep the calls short.

---

**Small businesses that use this successfully**

A business coaching company successfully filled the evening seminars they ran every quarter with a disciplined sales letter and follow up phone call approach. The phone call converted the people who were thinking about it, but needed a gentle nudge to take the step and book a place.

A monthly business club successfully recruits new members in the same way.

A fitness club follows up enquiries with a letter of introduction and a telephone call and finds that this method increases membership up-take by anything up to 50%.

A company selling plastic identity cards to universities find a letter of introduction along with a sample card and a follow up telephone call gets them successfully through to the appointment stage.

A training company uses telemarketing successfully to research prospects and book appointments. The telemarketing calls are followed up with an email introduction and, if appropriate, confirmation of an appointment.

---

**MAKING TELEMARKETING WORK FOR YOU – SPECIAL RESPONSE CHECKLIST**

▶ What are you going to use telemarketing for?

▶ Who is going to do it?

▶ Get your target prospect list.

▶ Set up your customer relationship management system.

▶ Decide on the purpose of the calls.

▶ Decide on how you are going to open the call and get the listener's attention.

▶ Prepare a list of relevant questions to ask.

▶ Set yourself some targets.

---

**Example prospect research questions**

The following questions could be applied or adapted to suit your business when using telemarketing to research for leads.

- Do you currently use ......... for $x$ and $y$?
- When do you tend to make your decisions about the suppliers you are going to use?
- How do you evaluate providers – what is the process you go through?
- What would we need to do to create the opportunity for you to see what we could do for you?
- What kind of problems do you have in the $x$ and $y$ area?
- What kind of solutions are you exploring?
- Are you interested in finding out more about how we could help?

---

## How to use this information

Take an element of your business where you consider telemarketing may help boost results and test it out. You will need to fine tune your approach until you get it absolutely right. Telemarketing is worth working at as it could give you the edge over others in your market.

> **Think telemarketing and get the
> business when others give up**

# 52 Getting people to pay attention to your window displays

## What is the purpose of a window display?

An attractive shop window display should draw passers-by to look and come in to buy. It is like an advert for your business that gives shoppers a taste of what they can expect inside. It is an opportunity to communicate your brand identity and stand out from neighbouring shops.

## Why is it important?

How many shop windows do you pass in a typical day? How many of them are using the space to their advantage? Many shoppers are attracted into a shop by what they see in the window. A good shop window display can get you more business. It is also free advertising.

Shops that are located close to traffic lights or road junctions where cars typically queue up really do have a captive audience. As your window display is the first thing people see when they pass by, it will influence their first impressions.

## Your challenge

A shop window will need to be dressed regularly for maximum impact. It will need to be colour co-ordinated and work with your existing image. It will take careful thought and planning every week if you want to get the most from it.

## How to create an attractive window display

- Go out and take a walk around your local town with the purpose of studying window displays. Note down anything you see that has impact.
- Make sure your shop facia is bold and reflective of your name and brand.
- Co-ordinate your colours.
- Make sure the sign and windows are always clean.
- Use special offers and new popular products, to attract attention.
- Organise your offers so that they can be seen and have impact.
- Keep it simple – do not clutter the display.
- Use vinyl window glass signage at the top, bottom or the side of the display.

- Keep your messages simple and straightforward.
- Update displays every week – give your customers something new to look at.
- You can use scrolling signs to attract the eye.
- You can use lights after dark to make your window display stand out.
- Don't leave grills or grates up or allow high reflective glass or poor lighting to make your shop look like it's not open.

A high street print, copy and design shop have found that their window display is their most effective marketing tool. They have a big glass frontage and are situated very close to a set of traffic lights with short queues round the clock. As soon as they realised that their window display was more important than any of their advertising they developed a complete strategy for making the most of it. It is so good at motivating new business that they have even been approached to sell advertising space on a scrolling banner in the window.

**MAKE THE MOST OF YOUR SHOP WINDOW – SPECIAL RESPONSE CHECKLIST**
- ▶ Look at your window display from the customers' point of view and ask yourself what your window display says about your business.
- ▶ Think about what you could do to maximise its impact.
- ▶ Measure the results you get by noticing what people are looking at and what they respond to.

## *How to use this information*

If you do have a business with a prominent window frontage it is well worth considering how you can use this information to make the most of it. Develop a long term strategy for marketing your business through the biggest advertisement you have.

> *Think of your shop window as an advert for your business*

# 53 Designing adverts that sell

## Why is this important?

Many people spend pounds on unplanned and poorly measured advertising and then find that they do not get the return they anticipated. Many are persuaded by the press to take late space or advertise in the latest feature and then find – because they rushed the design of their advert and made a spur of the moment decision – that it did not generate a result. This can be very frustrating and can result in a loss of faith in advertising as a method of attracting new customers. Many business owners make excuses for their lack of results by saying that they simply use advertising to keep their name out there. Advertising is very expensive if you do not get a result from it. There are many businesses generating thousands of pounds from advertising that works. They are the ones which have learnt how to design adverts that sell. They continually monitor and measure the return they get, fine tuning as they go. This is important if you want to get the best return from your advertising spend.

## Your challenge

Your challenge will be to make sure that any advertising that you do is targeted correctly. Any advert that you design will need to be designed to attract the right people. It will also need to appear in the right publication, which is one that is read by the highest number of your target prospects. You need to find out what the people you want to reach read, and where they go to research information about suppliers of the product or service that you are selling.

## For each publication you will need to consider

- Who reads it?
- Are the readers the people you want to reach?
- What are the readership or circulation figures?
- What geographical region does it cover?
- What are the planned features and how will they attract attention to your advert?
- Are there any specific sections that may naturally draw attention to your advertisement?
- Who else is advertising – what kind of responses and reactions did they get from their advert (people are often more than happy to share their experiences)?

## How to create an advert that sells – the AIDCA formula

Whenever you create an advertisement there are five essential key elements that follow the way a person psychologically responds to advertising both logically and emotionally. If you follow this formula when designing your advertisement it will give you the best chance of motivating your reader to respond.

The formula is easy to remember and easy to apply.

- **A** – It must attract **Attention** with the headline and the picture.
- **I** – It must keep the **Interest** by making it easy to read and understand.
- **D** – It must build **Desire** with the value, offers and benefits.
- **C** – It must **Convince** with a special offer, guarantee or testimonial.
- **A** – It must ask for **Action** by telling the reader how to respond and provide contact details.

These rules apply to any form of advertising that you do.

**YOUR ADVERT DESIGN – SPECIAL RESPONSE CHECKLIST**
- ▶ Who are you targeting? – describe your buyer.
- ▶ Decide what you want to sell to this buyer through this advert.
- ▶ Imagine that you are this buyer looking for information about this product or service – what would be the picture they have in their head? What information would they need?
- ▶ Choose an image that shows the buyer using or enjoying the product or service. Make it something that they can easily relate to.
- ▶ Think about what would get that reader's attention in the headline. This might be a special benefit, a new special offer, a short positive description of the product, a question that the target reader has to answer 'yes' to. You can also provoke curiosity by promising answers to questions they may have.

## Sample headlines

Let's imagine I want to attract new members to a golf and country club here are some examples of headlines that could attract the attention of the target audience

- Enjoy a challenging round of golf at the exclusive...
- The perfect round of golf.
- Calling all golfers...

- Do you want to spend more time playing golf?
- Three ways to improve your golf swing immediately.
- Do you want a *free* round of golf?
- Good news: golf club membership at special rates.

Consider the layout of the advert and how you can make it easy to read and follow.

Write a list of the benefits that this reader would get from the product of service. Write in a simple, straightforward way as if you were speaking to the reader telling them all about what is in it for them.

Decide what you are going to use to convince the reader and prompt a direct response from your advert. Give a special offer or guarantee.

What action do you want your reader to take? Tell them to call you, book a free consultation, or visit your showroom. Make sure that you have put all the correct contact details in your advertisement.

## *Sample advert layout*

| **Advert Sample Structure** |
| --- |
| **Picture:** Show the product or service being used and enjoyed |
| **Headline:** Attract the attention of the target audience |
| **Sub-headline:** Link the headline to the body copy and promise value |
| **Body copy:** Communicate your unique selling proposition and sell customer outcomes<br><br>Bullet points for strong emphasis<br>•<br>•<br>•<br>•<br>• |
| **Convince:** Include a special offer, guarantee or customer testimonial |
| **Action:** Ask customers to respond, tell them how and where to contact you |

## *How to use this information*

Take some of your existing advertising and run it through the AIDCA formula test. Step into your readers' shoes and see your offer through their eyes. Decide what could be improved and test it out. Monitor the results you get. Stop all advertising that is not bringing you a return. Make sure that you are targeting the right people through the right publications and if you have been guilty of making last minute decisions and placing haphazard adverts, stop it now. Make a commitment to design adverts that give you and your business the best possible chance of a positive return.

> *Think AIDCA and get more response*

# 54 Writing a good sales letter

## What is a sales letter?

A sales letter can introduce your product or services to potential customers. Its aim can be to pre-sell your service in advance of a follow-up sales telephone call. A sales letter can also stand alone as a 'sales person' in print and aim to do the complete sales task from start to finish. Sales letters can be sent direct mail or email.

## Why is it important?

A sales letter can be a valuable part of your sales and marketing process. Written well sales letters can persuade and influence your customers to buy, either directly from the letter or from you when you make your follow up telephone call. They allow you to target and communicate with more potential customers than you could physically talk to at any one time. Sales letters can warm customers up prior to a telemarketing campaign.

## Your challenge

Your challenge is to write a letter that gets read and responded to. Everybody receives so much mail these days in the post and via email that your letter needs to be good to stand out. Most of us scan letters very quickly and if nothing grabs our attention or stands out as being relevant and appealing then they tend to go straight in the bin.

## How to write letters that sell

*Know what your objective is*

Before you start typing you need to know what you want your letter to achieve.

*Know who you are targeting*

It is also important to be clear about who you are targeting and what their interests and problems are. This will help you to write copy that communicates directly with these people and provides solutions to their problems.

*Write as if you are writing to one person*

When you are writing put yourself into the shoes of the person you are writing to. Imagine that person as a friend and you are writing your message just for them. Even though this letter may go out to hundreds of people, each person will read it individually.

## Be personal – use 'you' and 'your'

If you include plenty of 'you' and 'yours' in your letter it will come across as if you are talking to the reader personally. You will be more likely to make a connection with the reader this way. Using 'you' and 'yours' shows the reader that you are focusing on them and their interests.

*Get the reader's attention from the start*

Headlines that communicate something immediately of value to the target reader will get their attention.

- A major benefit.
- A question that they have to say 'yes' to.
- An amazing fact or piece of research.
- Something new or different.
- An amazing opportunity.

The headline is the opening sentence and the first thing that is read. Use a spot colour to emphasise its importance.

*Make it look easy to read*

Readers will make a decision to read a letter or not very quickly. If the headline has successfully grabbed their attention and the letter looks easy on the eye there is more chance of it getting read. Short paragraphs with sub-headlines that highlight the main benefits, well spaced out will make the letter look attractive and pleasant to read.

*Write as you talk*

Imagine that you are going to have a conversation with someone and tell them all about the solution you have for them. Use easy to understand, plain English. Jargon and long words have the potential to bore and confuse. Be friendly and personable as if your were speaking to a friend.

### Keep your sentences short

Short sentences keep people's attention.

### Simplify

Eliminate excess wording. Be clear and concise in the points that you make. For letters you are sending in the post one A4 sheet is best. Scrolling email letters can be longer as long as the approach and language is kept simple and straightforward.

### Sell the benefits

Show that you understand the target readers' problems and explain the solutions you have for them. Talk about what your product or service can do for them and the outcomes they can expect to be satisfied. Make sure that you communicate your unique selling proposition.

### Include an action line

At the end of any letter you will want your readers to take a next step. You need to ask them to do that. If the next step to expect is a call from you within a defined time period then you must communicate that

### The power of a good PS

After the headline, the PS is the most read part of the letter, so you need to come up with a compelling PS. Your PS can be used to reinforce a key selling point or place some urgency on the response required.

### Proof-read

As your sales letter represents you and your business there is nothing worse than it going out with spelling or grammatical errors. It is best practice to get all your written sales and marketing materials double-checked by a professional proof-reader.

*Read aloud before you send*

When you read a letter you read it aloud in your head. Reading it aloud yourself once it has been completed is a great way of uncovering anything that doesn't quite work.

## The structure of a simple sales letter

**Dear** [name of person]

**Main Attention Grabbing Headline**

**Introduction**
Highlight target readers' problems

**Benefit-orientated sub-headline**
*Key sales points and solutions*

**Benefit-orientated sub-headline**
*Key sales points and solutions*

**Benefit-orientated sub-headline**
*Key sales points and solutions*

**Benefit-orientated sub-headline**
*Key sales points and solutions*

**Summary of main reasons to buy**

**Action line**

**Sign off**

**PS**

## How to use this information

Make sure that, if you are using a sales letter to pre-sell your services prior to a telecampaign, you make your call no more than three days after you send the letter.

Leave it longer than that and you risk the person forgetting about the letter no matter how well written it is.

If you have been using sales letters check them against the information you have here. How could you improve them?

> **Think sales letter and sell in print**

# 55 Using compelling direct mail

## What is direct mail?

Think of direct mail as a sales person in print sent directly to prospective customers by post in the form of a sales letter, flyer, brochure, post card or combination. Its purpose is to sell your products or services.

## Why is using direct mail potentially beneficial?

Here are some of the potential benefits of a compelling direct mail campaign.

- It leverages your efforts by getting your message out to thousands in one go.

- It allows you to target with precision by pinpointing the people who fit your psychographic, demographic and geographic profile.

- You can get an immediate response. If your campaign works, you will know about it quickly.

- It can work for you, selling your products and services while you sleep.

- It is a relatively low cost way of getting to large numbers of prospects.

- As it is tangible it can stay in your prospects' homes if they are interested but not ready to buy immediately.

## Your challenge

With all the mail that falls on most people's door mat in the morning there is a lot for any mail shot, letter or flyer to compete with. Most mail shots these days generate as little as a one per cent return. If the direct mail piece is not compelling for the receiver, then the chances are it will get put in the bin immediately. Sad, but true.

Direct mail can be a huge waste of time and money if you don't go about it in the right way. Sending out thousands of poorly targeted and poorly written mail shots is a bit like tipping a big bag of £5 notes down a drain. The sending of it does not guarantee a result. If you are serious about making your mail campaign work it will need some considered forethought and precision planning.

## Tips on how to get the best result from your direct mail

- Make sure that you send your direct mail to the right people. The key is to have the right mailing list to start with. You have the best chance of getting a response from people who have purchased something similar to what you are selling, people who have money to spend and belong to a group or organisation that have a strong want or need for your product or service. You can purchase mailing lists from list brokers who can help you to identify good lists for your direct mail campaigns.

- Sending a mailing to highly targeted prospects will raise your chance of success. If you are a landscape gardener and you send a mailing to owners of properties with large gardens in areas where there is disposable income, you will have a much better chance of a good response than you would sending it out to a housing estate with matchbox-sized gardens.

- Make sure that your direct mail follows the AIDCA formula already described.

- Use attention grabbers to get people to open it. Be creative and consider something a bit different or unusual that receivers can touch and feel.

- Personalise it if you can.

- Make your mailing look like a letter from a friend by printing your address labels in script or similar and avoiding colourful messages on the outside, which make it obvious that it is direct mail. The less obvious, the better.

- Sequential mailing campaigns get a better response than one-off mailings, as doing this well means that you are able to build a relationship with buyers over time.

- If you follow up a direct mailing with a telephone call you can increase your response rate by 50–100%.

- Don't send out more than you have the resource to follow up, as this needs to be done within a few days of sending the mail shot.

- Hand deliver and test. Another useful trick to getting a better return from your mail shot is to be selective about where you distribute it, and test small batches by hand delivering in the evenings.

- You can introduce your mail by voice broadcast over the telephone or by telemarketing: this can help to set up an expectation for it. Some organisations send competitions in the post as a way of attracting potential customers.

161

**YOUR DIRECT MAIL – SPECIAL RESPONSE CHECKLIST**

▶ What could you use direct mail for?

▶ Who are you targeting? – describe fully.

▶ Where can you get the best list of this target group?

▶ Check out list brokers.

▶ How are you going to approach it?

▶ Write your sales letter or direct mail flyer.

▶ Test it out on a few potential customers that you know – get some feedback?

▶ Set up your test batches and measure and monitor results.

▶ Fine tune your direct mail flyer or sales letter.

▶ Send out your campaign.

▶ Record your response results.

## *How to use this information*

If you think that there could be mileage in running a direct mail campaign, start small and learn as you go. There are lots of useful tips here that you can apply to any campaign large or small.

> *Think direct mail and get the right offer to the right door*

# 56 Using special offers and incentives

## What is a special offer?

A special offer is an opportunity for the customer to gain a financial advantage that is ideally perceived as irresistible. A special offer should motivate purchasing decisions because of the perceived value in it.

## Why are special offers important?

Special offers are as important to customers as they are to you. They can help you to achieve a number of things, for example: sell more, introduce customers to new products, speed up the buying cycle or move on old or unwanted stocks. Your customers also love a special offer. We are all motivated by an opportunity to get a good deal, something we want at a lower price than we would normally pay – a bargain!

Irresistible special offers are a great way to introduce new customers to your products or services and give existing customers a bonus.

## Your challenge

Your challenge is to make your offers so irresistible that your prospective customers say to themselves 'I really would be a fool to miss out on this opportunity', or ' I must take this opportunity right now or I will miss out'.

Your challenge is to do this in a way that motivates more new customers to try your services or buy your products.

## What makes a special offer successful?

When creating your special offers you need to understand the psychology of the 'risk – reward' thought process that goes on in the mind of your prospective customer.

Whenever someone considers buying anything they will naturally weigh up what they will get versus what they have to give to get those benefits. If the perceived risk is high and the perceived value is low, the chances are that the person will not buy. If the perceived risk is low and the value is high, then there is every chance more sales will be made.

So the best, most irresistible special offers are created when you increase the perceived value and lower the risk.

### Increase perceived value

Here are some ways to do this.

- Add in extra bonuses – e-book sellers are masters at this.
- Give two for the price of one or three for two – supermarkets do this well.
- Package complementary products together with a lower overall price compared to buying the products separately – spas and beauty salons are good at this.
- Detail why this product/service is special and unique and discount the price as an introductory offer.

### Decrease the perceived risk

- Give a strong guarantee.
- Provide low, affordable payment terms – most car retailers do this well.
- Offer interest-free credit – some furniture or electrical retailers do this well.
- Delay payments with no accrued interest – buy now pay later.
- Give free 30-day trial periods.
- Give access to follow up support after the sale has been made – computer software companies do this well.
- Prove a fast or large return on investment – property or financial investment companies do this well.
- Give proof of the results of the product or service using real life case studies.
- Endorse the product or service with testimonials.

If you combine a technique that increases perceived value with one that decreases perceived risk then you will enjoy an increased response rate to your special offer or incentive.

**HOW TO CREATE YOUR OWN SPECIAL OFFERS – SPECIAL RESPONSE CHECKLIST**
- ▶ What ideally would you like your special offer or incentive to achieve?
- ▶ What do you think would make an irresistible offer and attract new customers? Make a list of some of the options.
- ▶ Decide on the combination of increasing perceived value and decreasing perceived risk that would give your offer maximum leverage.

► Decide on a series of special offers and incentives to suit your own seasonal buying cycle.

► Decide how you are going to test your special offers.

► Find out by monitoring response rates what works and what doesn't.

## *How to use this information*

Integrate special offers and incentives into your sales and marketing strategy. Try different offers and test them out in your advertising, direct mail, email marketing, telesales, point of sale, networking events and talks and any marketing communication with new potential customers. Find the combination that works for you.

> **Think special offer and convert more sales**

# 12

# Profile building marketing

**inspiring ways
to market
your small business**

# 57 Getting free PR

## What is PR?

PR (short for Public Relations) is what you do to promote your business directly with the general public. You can do this through channels such as publishing articles on and off line, getting TV and Radio interviews, publishing press releases, giving talks, participating in charity events, getting involved with sponsorship and more. PR is about adding something to people's lives and in return you get good publicity.

There are many ways in which you can develop your own PR machine and in doing so get a lot of FREE positive publicity for your business.

There are publications, broadcast media, newsletters, newswires and websites within your marketplace that are always hungry for information and ideas.

Getting free PR is much easier than you think.

## Why is PR important?

PR is a vital piece of the marketing mix and especially powerful as it provides a natural third party endorsement for you personally and your products and services. It is your opportunity to position yourself as the industry expert, and get your name in the public eye. There are so many good opportunities out there that becoming good at getting PR can save you a lot in advertising spend.

## Your challenge

You will need to be selective. It could be very easy to spend all your time at it. The best PR for you will be that which targets your potential customers and gives you the chance to promote your business alongside it. You will need to build strong relationships with the editors and journalists of all publications and media channels relevant to your industry and marketplace. You will need to sell your ideas just as you would your products and services to a customer. Editors and journalists are interested in their readers and what they might find interesting and of value. Your challenge will be to present your ideas in a way that will appeal to their interests, not yours. PR is non-commercial. It is a softer way of communicating the great value you have to offer.

## *How to be successful at getting free PR*

*Articles*

The first thing that you can do is find out what the editors of all the industry press and websites are looking for.

They all produce regular feature lists and article writing guidance notes that explain exactly what you need to write in order to fulfil their criteria. It is then just a matter of adhering to their deadlines and sending in your articles. It always helps to have built up a relationship with the editor beforehand, so have a conversation about the article and angle you are planning, if possible. Offering an article series is a good way to build a continuous relationship with both editors and readers. An article series will really give you the chance to build a strong profile over time.

Suggesting an idea that is not in a feature plan is also a good approach. Find out what is a hot topic at the moment and then check out the publication article archives to see what has already been written on the subject to date. You then need to come up with a unique angle or something that will inspire readers.

Many magazines are interested in information that is backed up by some solid research data. If you are interested in generating some PR about a subject that you want the market to pay attention to, running a research survey and then offering the results as an article of interest is a very good way of achieving your goal.

*TV*

It is also possible to get opportunities to promote yourself on TV. Producers are always looking for new angles and ideas to boost audiences. Breakfast shows, national quizzes, central or local news, specialist shows and interviews could all be interested in your input and ideas. If you can provide something creative that would be of interest to the general public, and you can position yourself as the expert, then you would have a very good chance of getting an opportunity.

Think about the programmes on television recently where they have used an expert coach, consultant, trainer, or psychologist. The *National Quiz* shows, *Life Laundry*, *Fame Academy*, *Ten Years Younger*, a host of reality shows, *The Apprentice*, breakfast TV and more. Making contact with programme researchers will enable you to get inside information about the various shows which are being planned and, potentially, where the opportunities might be for you to help.

*Radio*

Radio interviews or call-in shows can provide another good PR opportunity. Contact the producers and find out what they have planned and if they are looking to interview any experts. You could suggest a call-in programme where listeners call in with questions that you answer live on air. Have a listen to some of the different radio stations and some of their live shows. This exercise might stimulate some ideas.

People care about what's important to them – things that will improve their life, improve their business, make money, save money, entertain them, fulfil them and protect them. Public relations will work for you as long as you keep your focus on what will benefit people's lives or businesses the most.

*Attract the press yourself*

If you are creative you can think about a high profile stunt or competition you could run in your local market area that would attract some press attention.

**CREATE YOUR OWN PR MACHINE – SPECIAL RESPONSE CHECKLIST**
- ▶ Consider your PR goals – what do you want to achieve?
- ▶ Consider the resources you have to manage your PR. Who can research the opportunities? Who can write articles? Who can take responsibility for placing them?
- ▶ What are the publications that your target audience read?
- ▶ What are the websites that they use?
- ▶ Where do they go to find out about potential suppliers in your marketplace?
- ▶ Where would you like to see your articles published?
- ▶ Consider what you could write about that would offer value to your target audience.
- ▶ How could you title or angle your articles to gain the attention of your target audience? 'How to' titles or lists of tips are popular ways to get readers' attention with the promise of value.
- ▶ How could you package the articles in a series?
- ▶ How could you position yourself as the expert? Make sure that you promote yourself well as the author of the article or participant in the PR exercise. Mention your position, organisation, qualifications (if relevant) and say something that refers to your expertise in the subject that you are referring to.
- ▶ How could you capitalise on any PR opportunity you get?
- ▶ Have you got any good ideas for an effective PR stunt?

## *How to use this information*

To make this work, you will need to take some time out to plan properly and investigate your PR campaign. You will also need to measure and monitor your return on investment: this will be the value you place on your own time. To do this well takes as much focus and thought as any other element of your business marketing plan. Once you have got the PR machine running and are happily generating a good return you will be glad that you took action.

> **Think PR and become more famous for what you do**

# 58 Writing and delivering press releases

## What is a press release?

A press release is a short, concise description of a potentially newsworthy story about your business. This is sent out to a selection of newspapers, magazines, and TV or radio stations to stimulate the interest of an editor or journalist in writing a full piece about it. The goal of a press release is to 'sell' your story. A press release can contain information about products, services, events, trends or almost anything.

## Why are press releases important?

Getting your press releases regularly accepted by all types of media outlets will give your business a free and very powerful marketing opportunity. Your potential customers, who read the press, watch TV and listen to their local radio stations could be influenced by your presence and your story. As a press release is read as someone else writing about your business, it will have more power than an advertisement which is produced internally. Press releases will certainly, over time, build your profile within your marketplace. If you can get into the national press you will benefit from the high coverage, as well as building credibility through association with the publication that publishes you.

## Your challenge

The bad news is that 99% of press releases are thrown in the bin, and a lot of those are written by PR agencies. So a lot of money is wasted. Your challenge is to get your press releases noticed and published. You can do this yourself once you know what to do and can follow a simple formula.

## What are the ingredients of a successful press release?

The good news is that those press releases that lead to a story or interview have certain qualities in common.

■ The best press releases step into the shoes of the journalist reading it, knowing that they are always searching for stories that are newsworthy and of reader interest.

■ They are targeted towards the needs or interests of the audience.

■ They are creative and offer something a bit different and original.

■ They are well written. Your release needs to be written in proper journalistic style, with short sentences and short paragraphs. Many journalists are looking for quick and easy stories that do not take up valuable time to prepare. A properly written press release can be published with little or no editing.

■ You must get it into the hands of the right journalists and editors. So do your research and know the correct name of the person to send it to.

■ Make sure you send the right release to the right publication.

## What kinds of press releases are likely to be newsworthy?

■ **Announcements** – new products, new management, merger, changes in corporate structure, partnerships, product changes, new equipment.

■ **Statements** – issue statements on topics that have an impact on your business. New legislation, for example.

■ **Events** – you can create a story about every event your company participates in. These may be events you send your team to, or ones that your company hosts. Speaking engagements, trade shows, special presentations or awards and community events that show you care are also of interest.

■ **Promote your customers** – write case studies showing how a particular customer accomplished a major goal because of your product or service.

■ **Accomplishments** – write about milestones that you have reached such as significant numbers of customers, years in business, expansions, new funding, new sales levels reached or awards won.

■ **Employees** – write about any good deeds your employees have done, achievements, community service.

■ **Charity** – if you get involved in charity events, promote the fact.

**WRITING A PRESS RELEASE – SPECIAL RESPONSE CHECKLIST**
▶ What is happening in your business right now that is newsworthy?
▶ Read the newspapers that you aspire to get into. See what kind of stories are getting in and notice the headlines they are using. Learn from them and angle yours in a similar way.

- Create a standard template for your press releases. Find out the names of all the journalists you need to send them out to, and then start a system of creating one newsworthy story every quarter and communicating it to them.
- When you have got an idea for a story you could test it out by calling one of the local newspaper journalists and asking whether it would be of interest and if so what kind of angle would get the best chance of publication.
- Generally speaking, journalists prefer not to get dozens of phone calls as their time is at a premium, however, at a local level it can work to your advantage if you can create the opportunity for a short conversation.
- Ensure that your press release headline is attention grabbing. Test some different headlines and their impact on getting accepted or not.
- Measure the results you get; notice what is getting in where.

## How to write a press release

- Your press release can be sent by letter, email or fax. Make sure that your name, full address and company details including full contact details are clear and obvious either up front or at the end.

- You also need to make sure that the editor is in no doubt what the communication is all about. So the words Press Release need to be in bold at the top of the page.

- If the release is for immediate release it needs to indicate that.

- Next will be the subject. You will need an attention-grabbing one-line headline.

- The summary should be one or two sentences that explain what the release is all about. Build your release with the most important information at the top. The release should not be the complete story, it is just the story idea that the journalist will develop.

- Keep the entire press release to one page only.

- End your press release with the basic information you want known about your company. This information can be used again in future releases.

- Mention any relevant pictures in the attachments section and then provide full contact details at the end.

Here is a sample structure for a press release:

---

> ### PRESS RELEASE
>
> To: *Editor's name, title of publication*
> From: *Your name, position and company*
> For immediate release
>
> Subject:
>
> Summary:
>
> Attachments:
>
> Organisation:
>
> Contact:

## *How to use this information*

Try it out. Create your first press release and send it out to your local newspaper and see how you get on. Taking action immediately is the only way you are going to find out if press releases are going to work for you.

> **Think press release and get the media attention you deserve**

# 59 Using banners, posters and signs

Your marketing messages can be promoted in many different situations by using a variety of banners, posters and signs.

Depending on whether you want to enhance your window display, make the most of your vehicles on the road, create a new look shopfront, provide direction inside and outside of your business, promote special offers or simply catch people's attention and communicate, good signage can help you do that. There are so many different types of promotional signage available to you on the market today. These are just some of the products available: vinyl banners, vinyl lettering, rotating banners, vehicle graphics, poster displays, builders' boards, rigid boards, swinging signs and more.

## What value do they offer?

Good business signage is important wherever you are located. Signs make it easy for people to see clearly where you are, what you do and what you are selling. A sign can be your business advertisement in the street. Signs, posters and banners can help you to increase your profile in your local area of business operation.

Vinyl banners can be used to communicate with visitors at both indoor and outdoor events, conferences, exhibitions or trade fairs. If you operate a service or trade business and are working on site, you can let people know who you are by putting up a banner or board. Passers-by could be looking for the service you are working on.

There are many relatively inexpensive places to put your banners and posters. Bus stops, roundabouts, billboards, notice boards and mobile advertising are just some of the many opportunities you can explore. You can rent field space from farmers with land near busy roads. Banner and poster advertising when positioned with care can capture the attention of passers-by.

Billboard, poster or mobile advertising in the same place for a defined period of time will capture the attention of regular passers-by or commuters. The more people see your message bold and bright in the same place, the more likely they will be to recall your name when they or someone they know needs your service.

## *Your challenge*

There are so many opportunities to use signs, posters and banners that you will need to make sure you choose what is right for your business. Too many can be as bad as too few. Everything you use to communicate your marketing message to your audience will influence their perception of you. If you use banners, posters and signs they will need to represent your brand and be designed to co-ordinate with your corporate theme. You will also need to be careful where you put them, being mindful of the image you wish to maintain. When it comes to signs with impact it is all about location.

## *What makes a good one?*

- Clear and easy to read.
- Well designed.
- Clean and colourful.
- Representative of your brand.
- Reflective of your corporate image.
- Strong visual impact.
- Attention grabbing headline.
- Strategically positioned to maximise impact on passers-by.

**YOUR USE OF BANNERS, POSTERS AND SIGNS – SPECIAL RESPONSE CHECKLIST**

- ▶ How easy is it for your customers to find their way to and around your business?
- ▶ Could better signage improve this?
- ▶ What about the vehicles you have on the road – are you maximising your advertising opportunity?
- ▶ Are there any roundabouts close to your premises that have a high throughput of traffic? Could you sponsor them?
- ▶ Which busy bus stops have poster slots available?
- ▶ Consider local mobile advertising. What is available and where?
- ▶ Are there any good billboard or poster opportunities locally?
- ▶ Look at your exhibition signage from the customers' point of view – does it really sell your business?
- ▶ Walk outside your premises and ask yourself if any space could be used to host banners or signage promoting your business.
- ▶ Think about your special offers or promotions and whether a swing sign, poster or banners could help you attract more attention.
- ▶ How could you make more use of banners, posters and signs?

## *How to use this information*

Banners, posters and signs could be a very useful way for you to build your profile, communicate with your customers and attract more attention to promotions. Consider the ideas presented and opportunities that exist for you to repeat your marketing messages until people really do remember you.

> **Think banners, posters and signs and make an IMPACT**

# 60 Exhibiting at conferences

## What are the potential benefits?

Exhibiting at conferences, business to business shows and exhibitions can be a great way to make direct contact with the key decision makers, buyers, owners, managers and directors of the organisations you want to influence. The people that are attracted to these events are information-hungry and time-poor and can often be difficult to reach via normal marketing channels. You will need to choose events that attract your target customer.

If you can speak and have a stand at a conference it will double your exposure and give you the best chance of generating leads, meeting customers face to face and ultimately developing new business.

Having a stand at an exhibition that targets the right market for you can be a great way for you both to launch and demonstrate new products and services. You will be able to show off your products and attract interest with live demonstrations and interactive presentations.

You will be able to network with both visitors and other exhibitors. You get the opportunity to talk to people, find out about their needs and interests. You can qualify your leads.

Many conferences and exhibitions offer a significant amount of market and media exposure prior to the event. They work hard to generate the audience for you. There will be opportunities for you to promote your business in advance of the event. There will be a dedicated conference or exhibition magazine, email updates and a special website.

Many exhibitions and conferences offer exhibitors and speakers the chance to publish their special conference offers and promotions in a voucher booklet designed to encourage visitors to seek them out at the event.

## Your challenge

Your first challenge will be to find an opportunity to exhibit at a conference that is most likely to target the audience you want to reach. Having found that opportunity and made the decision to have a stand, you will need to plan to make the most of it. It can be expensive if you do not take the necessary action to ensure you get a good return on your investment. You will need to be proactive in both your pre-conference activity, at the event itself and with your follow-up activities. Just being there will not be enough to get you the results you will need to make this a worthwhile marketing activity. There is a lot to think about to make a success of it.

## How to make a success of it

- Have a before, during and after plan.

- Organise a pre-conference promotion of your own to attract some of the key decision makers you have on your hot prospect list.

- If you are speaking at the conference use the opportunity to drive people to your stand with a promise of receiving something of value.

- Consider how you can ensure your stand makes an impact.

- Make sure that you have a good set of exhibition signs, display banners and posters that communicate clearly what you have to offer your visitors.

- Make sure that you are communicating your brand and that everything co-ordinates and reflects your image positively.

- Use pictures of people using and enjoying your products or service.

- Consider ways in which you can attract potential customers' contact details – you may run a competition, business card draw for an attractive prize, offer a free consultation or demonstration that requires entry via the person's contact details.

- Offer some attractive refreshments at your stand – everyone offers sweets, could you offer something different?

- If your business lends itself well to a short talk, presentation or demonstration run this at set times of the day and use it to attract a crowd.

- Engage your audiences' senses – sight, sound and touch – consider how you could give them an experience of your product or service.

- Make sure that you have a number of good giveaways that promote your service well.

- When information-gathering visitors ask for brochures, make sure that you identify their interest by asking some questions and get their contact details.

- Make sure you have a good brochure and enough business cards to give away on demand.

■ Give your visitors a chance to browse and make your contact with them natural. The people who visit your stand often don't want to be pounced on the minute they arrive.

■ Make sure whoever is working your stand enjoys communicating with people.

■ Dress smartly.

■ Have fun.

■ Follow up your leads within a week of the conference.

**THINKING ABOUT EXHIBITING – SPECIAL RESPONSE CHECKLIST**

▶ What are you hoping to achieve by attending this conference?

▶ Why is the conference you have chosen likely to be good for your business?

▶ What kind of return on your investment will you need for this to have been a success?

▶ How can you attract some of your own key customers to your stand?

▶ Step into a typical visitor's shoes – what might their interests be in your product or service? What could be attractive to them?

▶ Who is going to manage the stand and what is your strategy?

▶ How are you going to generate leads?

▶ How are you going to follow up?

## How to use this information

If you are new to exhibiting and, having read this section, are considering doing so, you will need to do your research. Find out about some conferences and exhibitions that target the kind of people you want to reach. Attend yourself as a visitor and check it out. Find out if any similar businesses to yours are going to be there. Have a chat with them about their experiences and find out how productive they have found the event.

If you are already a seasoned exhibitor there may be some ways that you could improve your approach in order to maximise the return you get from it.

> **Think exhibit and make a stand for yourself**

# 61 Becoming a well known expert in your field

## *What is an expert?*

An expert is a person who has a high level of skill and knowledge in a particular niche area. An expert is someone who is seen to have a specific talent and extensive experience in one particular field. Experts are often thought of as the best problem solvers and solution providers in their field. They are the leading authorities whose knowledge people trust.

## *Why is becoming one important?*

Becoming an expert and promoting yourself as one is a very good way to ensure that you gain the maximum trust and recognition in your industry. People love experts and would much rather pay more for someone who is known as the best in the business. Imagine if you wanted to explore the possibility of franchising your business, who would you rather take on as a consultant to advise you on the best way forward, a franchising expert or a generalist? Who would you be prepared to pay more for? Who would you be most likely to recommend to others who wanted a similar solution? The expert wins every time.

When you focus in on a specific niche area and become the resident expert you will find yourself seeing the same problems over and over again. Eventually you will create a set of solutions that can be applied to 90% of the problems your clients face. You will build up more and more success references. Over time this will give you more and more authority. Once people see you as someone who really does understand their needs and problems and has proven methods and ideas to help them, they will buy your services confidently. Developing an intimate knowledge of specific problems and having solutions that work is very powerful indeed.

## *Your challenge*

Your challenge will be in deciding to be the expert and focusing on a specific area of business. Many people are afraid to specialise and pride themselves of being able to provide their clients with anything and everything. Deciding what you are going to be the expert in will take research and forethought. You will need to find the problems first and design your expertise to provide the solutions. Specialising takes concentration and commitment. Creating an expert status in the marketplace needs a strategy all of its own.

## *How to be seen as an expert*

- Describe your expertise in a way that shows people how you can solve their problems.
- Build a portfolio of testimonials and references for your work.
- Work in a targeted, narrow field solving specific problems for specific people.
- Target the promotion of your expertise to the people who need you most.
- Get a book published and share your expertise.
- Write articles for business publications and websites.
- Get on TV or radio shows as the resident expert.
- Run open events and seminars connected with your area of expertise.
- Join associations and professional institutes that verify your expert status.
- Speak at conferences connected with your area of expertise.
- Complete continued professional development and build your expertise through experiences.
- Build your word of mouth and referral marketing.
- Give ideas away – create a free newsletter or information sheet.

**ARE YOU AN EXPERT? – SPECIAL RESPONSE CHECKLIST**
You may already be an expert. Find out by answering the following questions.

- What are your greatest talents and skills?
- What are the most important problems you solve for people with these talent and skills?
- What advice do people come to you for most often?
- What have you been asked to speak about at conferences?
- What kind of expertise do your clients value?
- What level of expertise is expected in your business?
- How can you prove your expertise?

## *How to use this information*

You can create and promote expertise in any business. If you can see, having uncovered your own expertise, that you have something that your customers would value, you owe it to the world to let people know about it. Get out there and shout about it.

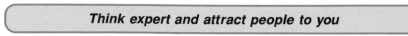

*Think expert and attract people to you*

# 62 Sponsoring for maximum return

## What is sponsorship?

Sponsorship is when your business enters into a mutually beneficial relationship with a person, event or activity that enables you to connect your brand with the audience it attracts. You as a sponsor will provide an agreed sum of money that will allow you an agreed set of promotional opportunities.

Each sponsorship deal will be different depending on what it is and what it involves. Sponsorship opportunities exist in the arts and media, sport, business and in the community. They exist at all levels from local to global. The investment required can also range from a few hundred to thousands of pounds depending on the perceived value of the marketing opportunity.

For the small business there are many local opportunities to connect your business with worthwhile events, competitions and people that attract attention. Some examples might be business awards, school and community projects, football matches, conferences, business shows, social events, festivals, charity auctions, horse shows, polo matches, cycling competitions, boat races and many more.

## Why is It of value?

The potential value of sponsorship is in its potential for connecting your brand with the values and interests of the audience that the sponsorship targets. Sponsoring an event can help your potential customers to make an emotional connection with your business as a direct result of your involvement in an event or sport that matters to them. Sponsorship can enhance the relevance of your product or service to your audience if the opportunity is used to provide some customer education. The attributes of your brand can be connected with the attributes of the event.

Sponsorships can create an opportunity for you to make more impact with your existing marketing activities. You can promote your connection with the event and the event will promote its connection with you.

Sponsorship is about building a better and more loyal relationship with your existing and potential customers.

## *Your challenge*

Choosing the right event or person to sponsor will be your challenge. Sponsorship can be no different to giving someone a cash handout if you do not plan to achieve something from it. Spur of the moment decisions based on gut instinct with no particular objective are most likely to result in nothing more than a warm feeling.

If you want to maximise the return you get, you will need to have a plan and a strategy for doing so in the same way as you would have for any other marketing activity you engage in.

## *How to sponsor for maximum return*

- Make sure that you know what you want to achieve with your sponsorship. Is it about raising your profile, educating customers, generating leads, building customer loyalty or making a connection and association with something your target audience cares about?

- Make sure that you are very clear about who your target audience is and what their interests are. If you want to target young people who enjoy socialising, then you might consider sponsoring a local beers and blues festival. If you want to target successful small business owners, then you might consider sponsoring the local business awards competition. If you want to target horse owners, you might consider sponsoring a show jumping competition at a county show.

- Know your own brand values and what kind of event would enhance those values. If your brand is about prestige or fun and creativity then the event you choose must reflect those values. Sponsoring the wrong event can be damaging to your brand.

- Do your research. Find out about the sponsorship opportunities available to you. Discuss the audience profile, numbers and values. Make a match with a sponsorship opportunity that best fits with the people and values you wish to connect with.

- Make sure that you get your team's buy-in to the sponsorship. Getting their support and involvement will be the key to making the complete relationship work.

- Plan how you can integrate the sponsorship you have committed to into your current marketing and promotional activities.

- Decide on a sponsorship budget and stick to it.

■ Decide how you will know if your sponsorship has been successful. Consider what measures you can you put in place.

**CONSIDERING SPONSORSHIP? – SPECIAL RESPONSE CHECKLIST**

▶ What do you want to achieve?

▶ What type of events would help you build a stronger connection with your target audience?

▶ Where do your target audience go – what do they support?

▶ What does your brand need to be associated with?

▶ Having short-listed some events – what are the potential benefits of each?

▶ Consider how you could use your sponsorship opportunity to offer customer education.

▶ How would you like your business represented at the event?

▶ What promotional messages would be appropriate to accompany the sponsorship activity?

▶ How could you add value at the event and make yourself memorable?

▶ What creative ideas do you have for using the sponsorship opportunity to generate some leads? Is there something you could offer that would get people to contact you?

▶ What involvement do you want your team to have?

▶ What is your plan to maximise your return on your investment?

## How to use this information

Maybe you have sponsored before but not really considered how you could maximise the return you get from it, or maybe you are considering it for the first time. Either way, sponsorship can be one of the best ways of building a strong and loyal connection with your target audience. Use this information to help you plan your approach. Get it right for your business brand and the customers you want to influence.

> **Think sponsorship and make a connection
> with your target audience**

# 63 Giving something back to society

## What is giving back?

Giving back is when you do something for the society that you live in and do business in genuinely to help people. This activity should not be profit related. Giving back is about sharing your success with others less advantaged than you. Examples of how you might do this could be donating a percentage of your monthly profits to a special charity, offering your skills or service to educate or inform under-privileged groups of people, offering an educational opportunity to state-funded schools or donating products to people who you know would benefit from them but are unable to afford them.

## Why is it important to do this?

The activity of giving back is important to the soul of your business. Those important values of care, consideration and awareness of those less fortunate are fundamental to the spiritual growth of your business. If you give a little you will receive a lot. People also like to associate themselves with businesses that support causes and disadvantaged people in a meaningful way. If you do this it can bring you closer to your customers.

## Your challenge

Running a small business and striving to make it a success can take all your energy and focus. It can be easy to get lost in the drive for results and forget the importance of giving back. Your challenge is to remember and, if you believe it is important, find something you and your business can do that would benefit others that has nothing to do with promoting yourself or making money. It can be refreshing to think like this sometimes.

## How to give back

Find something that you can do that means something to you and your organisation. Look for a charity that you can support with which you have some affinity. Look for a business enterprise or state-funded organisation that needs the services that your business offers. Marketingco has worked with a local enterprise council that runs business enterprise days in local schools. I have run educational introduction-to-marketing sessions for school-children. This was fun for us to do as well as being of great interest to the pupils. Breast cancer charities and the protection league for horses are charities that we support because of the special affinity we have with them. Find a worthy cause that resonates with you and your team. Find a situation where your skills could be of great value.

You don't have to give much to give back. The act of giving is enough. In many situations only £5 a month will feed or clothe a whole family in a third world country or save an animal. You also don't have to wait until you are successful to give back. Give as you are growing as a business as a way of showing how you mean to go on. Give in accordance with the rate of your success.

**WHAT IS RIGHT FOR YOU AND YOUR ORGANISATION – SPECIAL RESPONSE CHECKLIST**
- ▶ Brainstorm ideas with your team.
- ▶ What charities do people have a connection with?
- ▶ What kind of charities would resonate with your type of business?
- ▶ What is going on at the moment in the world that you could support?
- ▶ Where would a donation of your products make a BIG difference?
- ▶ What kind of local, national or global organisations need your support now?
- ▶ How could you involve your customers in helping you find new ways to give back?
- ▶ How could you use your own marketing activities to gather more support?

## How to use this information

There are potentially hundreds of opportunities to help others. Organisations are always looking for special businesses to help them in their cause. Search them out and offer your helping hand.

> **Think give back and show your values in action**

# 13

# Selling your services

**inspiring ways
to market
your small business**

# 64 Opening a cold call

Making direct contact with your prospects by telephone can be a good way to research sales opportunities and set up sales appointments.

Many people have a fear of cold calling and this can get in the way of using this potentially powerful way of generating good sales leads.

## Make a cold call warmer

It can make it a lot easier to open a new telephone call when you are following up a letter or email of introduction.

## What do you want to achieve?

To start with it is much more useful to think about these calls as research as opposed to cold calls. The word 'cold' infers that the person you are calling is likely to be cold with you. Not a pleasant thought! What you are doing is using the telephone contact as a way of finding out if there is someone who has a problem or requirement that potentially could be solved by your service. You will not be using the telephone for any more than setting up a face-to-face or telephone appointment with a decision maker. Not thinking that you have to sell something can take the pressure off and make opening a call much easier.

## Get the name of the decision maker

It is important to find out in advance who the right person to speak to is. You can do that very easily by making a separate call to the organisation and asking very politely if the reception team or department member can help you. Be very clear what the responsibilities are of the person's name you want. Give a good reason for asking for the person's name. Once you have the correct name and title of the person you can make your call on a separate occasion.

## Opening the call from your prospect's point of view

Imagine that you are standing in your target prospect's shoes for a moment and living a typical day in their busy business life. Most people are distracted when their phone rings, their mind is on other things. You will need to show that you understand their position and can provide a good reason for them to listen.

So how do you do that?

> Good morning/afternoon [name of person you have been put through to as the decision maker] my name is [your name] from [our company name]. I understand that you are the person who manages/deals with [add the area that is important to your call]. Have I called at a convenient time? (If not, arrange to call back.)

At this stage the person you have called does not know why you have called so asking if you have called at a convenient time is common courtesy and will show them that you have some empathy with the pressures of their work load.

Once you have their ear you will have an opportunity to explain again who you are and what the purpose of your call is. Be straightforward, up front and honest.

> My name is Jackie Jarvis from Marketingco; I am calling to follow up a letter I sent you last week. We work with small to medium sized businesses helping them to make their marketing work. I don't know at this stage if you are currently looking for help in this area, but I wanted to follow up and find out if you might be interested in our free one hour consultation.

The following approach may work if you have not sent a letter in advance.

> We are looking for organisations which are interested in [mention a generic need or experience you can fulfil or solve] that we may be able to provide/solve. I have no idea if this is something that you are exploring at the moment, but I though I would call to find out. Is this something you have on your agenda right now or are likely to have in the future?

## *Find out if you have a business prospect*

Create the opportunity to ask a couple of quick questions to establish if the person you have called is, in fact, a prospect.

What you ask will depend on the business you are in and what you need to know about the person on the end of the phone to establish whether or not they are a prospect. Choose your questions wisely and find out as quickly as you can if they have potential.

You may need to ask the person if they currently use $x$ product or service. If so, do they have anything that they need at the moment? Are they looking for any of the solutions you have or are they experiencing any of the challenges you describe?

You may need to find out the process they go through to choose suppliers and whether they are open to meeting with you at some stage. You will need to close the call by arranging the appropriate follow up activity.

The result of the call may be

- an appointment
- another opportunity for a longer telephone consultation
- a note on your CRM system to call back at some stage in the future when a demand is more likely to exist
- no we are not prospects.

Then thank the person for their time and their information and confirm any follow up you have arranged by email.

## How to use this information

Use the basic structure of the call as outlined in this section and consider how you could adapt it to suit your products and services. Try it and monitor what works and what doesn't.

> **Think research and make your cold calls warm**

# 65 Making appointments

## Why are appointments important?

Sales appointments are your opportunity to get in front of your potential customers face to face and explore how you may be able to help them. Having agreed to an appointment with you, your prospect has taken the first step forward, a move that says 'yes, I want to know if you have a solution for me'. Getting to that stage in the sales process gives you that important opportunity to find out first hand what their needs are. It is much easier to do that face to face than it is over the telephone or by email.

## Your challenge

Your challenge will be to make sure that the sales appointments you set up are with properly qualified decision makers. You can waste a lot of time, money and effort making appointments with poorly qualified people who cannot make a decision to go ahead.

## Ways to make appointments

### Using the telephone

You can make appointments as explained in the previous section by telephone prospecting. You may need to go through a number of stages before an appointment becomes appropriate. This may require a number of telephone follow ups, and the provision of information about your product or service.

### Networking

Appointments can also be made when you meet a potential prospect at a networking event, business conference or exhibition. A brief exchange with someone may create an opportunity to suggest a further more private conversation to discuss their needs in more depth. This can be kept casual and informal initially.

### Entice with the offer of a free consultation

The offer of a free consultation, product demonstration or business health check can be a way of giving your prospect something of value with no pressure to buy.

This can motivate them to see you face to face. Having created this opportunity you can start to build a relationship with them. I offer a free marketing consultation as the first step in my appointment-making process. The consultations last for one hour and are held at our private meeting room. I offer the free consultations whenever I speak at networking events, run seminars or write articles. I also promote the consultations on our website. Not all the people who take up the free consultation become clients immediately. It does, however, start a relationship with a potential client which could lead to further business in the future.

There are many examples of small businesses that use this kind of approach to generate appointments. A financial consultant offers a free personal finance assessment and reports back, a health and safety consultant offers a free health and safety check with a report highlighting *must dos*, *should dos* and *could dos*, a website marketing company offers a free 'how well marketed is your site' report that highlights all the areas for improvement. These are all the kind of reports that potential customers find valuable. They can learn something about themselves and their business.

Make your recommendation for an appointment sound like an opportunity for your prospect.

**HOW PRODUCTIVE IS YOUR APPOINTMENT MAKING? – SPECIAL RESPONSE CHECKLIST**
- How do you make appointments?
- How successful are you at pre-qualifying your prospects?
- How successful are you at getting appointments with key decision makers?
- How could you attract more people to request an appointment from you?
- How could you make your appointment recommendations seem like an opportunity for your prospect?
- How could you improve your appointment-making process?

## How to use this information

Consider what you can do to utilise these ideas to help you and your team get more appointments.

**Think appointment and convert more prospects to customers**

# 66 Building instant rapport

## What is rapport?

Rapport exists when two or more people find that they have a mutual understanding, share some values, ideals or experiences and as a result can communicate easily. When you have rapport it usually means that there is a connection between you and another person. This connection can happen at different levels over different time periods. From a sales point of view, the more instant the rapport the better. Having a rapport usually means that both parties like each other. You don't have to like someone to be able to do business with them, but it helps if you do. Different levels of rapport will exist with different people. You wouldn't expect each and every customer you meet to share the same level of rapport you have with your best friend. You would expect to create an appropriate level of rapport with the people you do business with.

## Why is it important?

Your ability to work successfully with people or sell your services to them will be influenced greatly by the level of rapport you are able to build. The more rapport you have, the easier it will be to build good business relationships. When you think back to your own experiences of doing business, have you ever chosen to do business with someone that you didn't have any rapport with? Have you ever chosen to work with someone because you felt they liked and understood you?

Rapport is the oil that lubricates all good human relationships. Without its presence it can be hard work – with it, everything can be so much easier.

## Your challenge

You may meet a lot of people in a typical month in your business. You won't be able to create the same level of rapport with all of them. There will be people you come across who are so different from you that you may struggle to build a connection. Your challenge will be to become interested in those people who are different to you and find some common ground. This common ground is the bedrock that supports rapport.

## How to build instant rapport with the people you want to sell your services to

- Start conversations by finding some common ground.
- Share something appropriate about yourself as a person.
- Put yourself in their shoes. Consider what their outcomes are.
- Really get to know them as a person, get interested in their life, challenges and goals.
- Be open-minded and decide to find something to like about each person you meet.
- Really, genuinely care about helping them to succeed.
- Be aware of how they are responding to you.
- Find out exactly how they need you to help them. Find out what they want.
- Make the person feel important and show that you care.
- Pace and match body language and voice tone.
- Laugh together and create a positive state.

**HOW GOOD ARE YOUR RAPPORT BUILDING SKILLS? – SPECIAL RESPONSE CHECKLIST**

- What does having a good rapport mean to you?
- How do you know when you have rapport with someone?
- How do you know when you don't have rapport?
- Which of your clients do you have the best rapport with?
- What kind of people do you find it harder to build rapport with?
- What do you do to ensure you build rapport with new prospects?
- Would a better rapport help you to do more business?
- What could you do to improve your rapport-building skills?

## How to use this information

People who are good rapport builders usually attract new business much more quickly and easily than people who aren't. It is worth considering your own rapport-building skills and what you can do to fine tune them.

> **Think rapport and build stronger business relationships**

# 67 The art and power of listening

## What is listening?

Being listened to is very important to most people. It is a sign of respect and genuine interest. True listening happens when a total focus on the speaker exists. What they are saying and feeling is heard and understood. There are no distractions nor any misunderstandings based on the listener's own interpretation or perception. Those who are skilled listeners will hear more than just the words. They will hear the speaker's

- reality
- concerns
- opinions and perceptions
- beliefs
- feelings and emotions
- desires
- needs.

They will also be aware of the non-verbal communication of body language and voice tone and pace. Good listeners are able to get to the core of what matters most to the person they are in contact with.

## Why is it important?

Really listening to your clients will enable you to find out not just what they might need, but what they really value and who they are as people. Everyone likes to be recognised for who they are, as well as being paid individual attention. This is what the best relationships are made of. Being an excellent listener is a rare skill and, of course, is one of the greatest rapport moves.

Can you remember the last time you were really listened to? As you remember that time, can you recall how it felt to have someone's total focus and attention and know that listening to you was really important to them?

## Your challenge

Your own perceptions, judgments and the conversations you have inside your own head can act as a block to what is being said by the person who is speaking to you.

You may miss what matters most to them. Allowing yourself to become distracted or being too keen to move the conversation on to where you want it to be will get in the way.

Listening can be a selfless activity. You will need to relax and be in the right mental and emotional state yourself to be able to give your full attention.

## How to listen

Good listening starts with making a decision to give the person speaking your full and undivided attention. Get yourself into a listening state by preparing yourself beforehand. If you have been busy and have a lot on your mind, give yourself ten minutes to clear your head and relax.

- Arrange a place to meet that is free from distractions and is quiet and calm. Arrange seating at a round table or around the corner of a desk or table. Turn chairs towards each other with enough personal space between you to enable you to hear, but not crowd, each other.

- Make sure that you look at your speaker, ask relevant questions and summarise from time to time to check your understanding of what they are saying to you.

- Notice your speaker's responses, pick up on their language and where appropriate feed it back to them. This will make the person feel heard.

- Notice the energy, tone and pace of the speaker's voice. Match that energy and pace when you ask questions and summarise. This will help you to maintain rapport and again make your speaker feel heard.

- Check your understanding and interpretation of their issues from time to time during the conversation and if you need clarification, ask for it.

- Make sure that you are able to communicate exactly what their priorities are and what matters to them in any follow-up proposal.

**HOW GOOD ARE YOUR LISTENING SKILLS – SPECIAL RESPONSE CHECKLIST**
- ▶ Think of a time when you were really able to listen to someone – what did you do?
- ▶ Think of a time when you were not able to listen to someone well – what was the difference?
- ▶ Who would say that you are a good listener?
- ▶ Who would say that you weren't?

▶ In what situations do you listen?

▶ In what situations do you find it difficult?

*Do you ever*

▶ Get distracted when someone is talking?

▶ Interrupt the conversation with one of your own opinions, ideas or stories?

▶ Let your mind drift whilst the person is talking?

▶ Look at your watch whilst a person is talking?

▶ Misinterpret or misunderstand what someone has said?

▶ Switch off?

▶ Ask irrelevant questions?

What do you think that you need to do to improve your ability to listen?

What impact do you think better listening would have on your sales appointments?

## How to use this information

If, having read this section, you recognise that your own listening skills could improve, the first stage would be to start to become aware of what happens to you when you are listening to people. Notice what goes on in your head, your physical and emotional state and your own listening or non-listening behaviours. Make a conscious decision to listen more and notice what impact that has on your relationships with clients and colleagues.

> *Think listen and really hear what is being said*

# 68 Getting to your prospect's pain – the questions to ask

## What is your prospect's pain?

People buy to fulfil outcomes and to solve problems with solutions. People who are in the market for certain products and services often have a problem that they need an answer to. Your prospect's 'pain' will be the real reason they are in the market-place looking for a solution. The pain a prospect has will not usually be the first thing that they tell you when they meet. You will need to uncover it with questions and then show them how you are able to make the pain go away with your product or service.

## Why is it important to find it?

The real painful issue behind your prospect's desire to find a solution will be the light that will ignite their desire to buy. If you can find it you will be in a stronger position when describing your solution. You are more likely to motivate a person to buy from you when they see that you understand what they really want and why they want it.

## Your challenge

Your challenge will be to ask the right questions and build enough trust and rapport between you and your potential customer so that they feel comfortable enough to tell you what you need to know. You will need to get their permission to probe. You will also need to listen, summarising for clarification at key intervals.

## Questions to ask which find the pain

- What do you need to find out about $x$ or $y$?
- What is most important that you find out about this $x$?
- Why is that most important to you?
- When choosing $x$ or $y$ what matters most?
- What are your priorities?
- What problems have you been experiencing that has led to a desire to explore $x$?
- What led you to decide to look for an $x$ solution?
- What has motivated your need to find a solution for $x$?

- What has been most challenging for you?
- How do you hope we can help you?
- What do you feel that you really need to achieve $x$?
- What are your timescales?

**FIND THE PAIN – SPECIAL RESPONSE CHECKLIST**

▶ What are some of the problems people have that motivate a desire to buy your product or service?

▶ What kind of pain drives their decisions?

▶ What kind of questions would uncover this pain?

## How to use this information

The first part of any sales appointment should be all about the prospect. You will need to have a good set of questions that enables you to both uncover their pain, find out what they need, what their priorities and timescales are.

Once you have summarised your complete and full understanding of their position you will be in the best place to position your solution. Use this section to help you to create a targeted set of consultation questions.

> *Think prospect's pain and sell more gain*

# 69 Tailoring your sales proposition and positioning the benefits

## What is a sales proposition?

A sales proposition is your presentation of a solution. A solution that potentially solves the problems and needs you have established during the exploratory part of your sales conversation. Your sales proposition may take the form of a presentation, proposal, dialogue or all three. The method you choose to use to communicate your sales proposition will depend on what is most appropriate.

## What is meant by positioning the benefits?

Positioning the benefits is all about making a connection or link between what is important to your prospect and what you are able to fulfil. Positioning the benefits is about telling or showing exactly what your solution will do for your prospect. Benefits bring the solution alive and sell the value.

## Why is it important?

Tailoring your sales proposition and positioning the benefits is how you ensure that your prospect lives the full potential value of your solution. It is so much better than just running through the generic facts. Your prospect will be interested in their needs, their problems and their solution. They will want to feel special. Tailoring your proposition and using their language to do that is a very powerful way of ensuring that you hit all the right buttons. The greater the fit, the greater the chance you will have of getting a positive reaction.

## Your challenge

To tailor your sales proposition and position the benefits effectively you will need to be very clear about what the benefits of your solution are in the first place. Listening and asking the right questions will have been a vital part of the process. Without having the correct information about your prospect's needs, problems and values it will be impossible to tailor your proposition. You will also need to be flexible and able to communicate what you do for people in different ways. You will not be able to rely on a standard sales pitch. Each presentation you make might be slightly different from the one before.

## *How to tailor your sales proposition for each individual client*

- Summarise your prospect's present problems and desired outcomes.

- Use their language.

- Make sure that you have their full agreement on their issues.

- Take each separate need or group of needs and connect with a description of a solution for them. Tell them exactly what you can do to help them to achieve what matters most.

- Project into the future by relating the solution you are suggesting to the bigger picture.

- Share relevant examples of how you have helped organisations to solve similar problems and achieve a good result. Make sure that you choose examples that the prospect will relate to.

- Make your recommendations confidently.

**CAN YOU IMPROVE YOUR SALES PROPOSITIONS? – SPECIAL RESPONSE CHECKLIST**
▶ How do you tend to make your sales propositions?
▶ How well do they work?
▶ Do you tailor your sales propositions?
▶ Are you communicating more about what your prospect will get than what you do?
▶ What can you do to improve your sales propositions?

## *How to use this information*

After you have communicated your sales proposition you will want to get to a point when your prospect says 'Yes I want to do business with you'. If you can reach this point conceptually after a verbal presentation, your final stage will be a proposal and the price. If you have been able to gauge budgets and price expectations during your initial conversations it will make it a lot easier to position the price in your ultimate proposal.

> *Think benefit and get the business*

# 70 Designing a winning proposal

## What is a proposal?

A proposal is your summation of exactly what your client will get for their money. You will usually only prepare a proposal after you have gained conceptual agreement to work with the client. This may follow an initial appointment during which you will have explored what the client's problems, needs and priorities are. You may also have explored the budgets they would be comfortable working within. Your proposal can be delivered in either electronic, hard copy presentation or both. Even better, you can deliver in person giving you another chance to get in front of them. Your style of delivery will very much depend on the individual client's expectations and the nature and value of the work you are proposing.

## Why is it important?

It is important to make a good job of your proposal as even though your potential client has agreed conceptually, the deal will have not been finalised. Your prospective client may use the proposal to make their final decision. They may want to compare your proposal with others. Your proposal will show them how well you have listened and understood their position and requirements. It represents you, your organisation and resells the potential value of the solution before the final commitment is made to your proposal.

## Your challenge

Your challenge may be that you have a lot of very time-consuming proposals to prepare. If, as a result, your proposal is late and lacking in any way, you risk giving your prospect a negative message about your reliability or ability to meet the required standards the job requires. Your proposal and everything that goes with it is a reflection of you and what your business promises. It can make or break the final outcome.

Never do a proposal on speculation. It will waste your time and you won't have enough information to make a good job of it.

## The structure of a winning proposal

It is a good idea to create a basic proposal template that covers the key sections important to your proposal. You can add in the individual customer's detail as required. This will make it a lot easier and quicker to do. There may be elements of your proposal that end up as standard. Your proposal will need to provide enough detail for your client to make their decision. It will also need to look attractive and be easy to read and interpret. Section headings that include the word 'Your' will make it appear very personal.

## The key elements of a winning proposal will include

- **Introduction** – Refer to your last meeting along with an overview of what to expect in this proposal.

- **Your situation** – This is your situation summary of what you established was important at your recent meeting. Use their language, priorities and timescales.

- **Your objectives** – Bullet point exactly what they have told you.

- **Your solution** – The solution you suggest broken down so that the client can see all the key elements clearly. You may include in this section some standard descriptions of elements of your service, product and methodology you propose.

- **Value** – Make sure that the ultimate value of each element of the solution is communicated. What is in it for them is most important. They are buying results, not processes. It may be appropriate to refer to financial savings or other tangible results they will benefit.

- **Your price** – An outline of your charges and any price assumptions. If you have price guarantee this is the time to include it.

- **Your plan** – This could include suggested targets and timescales. A calendar of actions is a useful way of projecting forward, assuming the project will go ahead.

- **Your next step** – This is where you suggest the follow up you have agreed.

- **Sign off** – a positive statement about working together in the future.

## Success tips

- Make sure that you fully understand your client's situation before you do your proposal.
- Don't make it too long: two or three pages is enough.
- Keep the language you use straightforward and clear.
- If you can, provide your client with a choice of options.

■ If you outline your methodology keep this broad; too much detail and you give all your secrets away.

■ Always follow up yourself – don't leave it longer than a week.

### HOW GOOD ARE YOUR PROPOSALS – SPECIAL RESPONSE CHECKLIST

▶ Take time out to have a good look at the standard of your own proposals.

▶ How long, on average, do they take you to complete?

▶ Do you get them out on time?

▶ How many of them turn into new business? How many don't?

▶ How well do they reflect the image you want to portray to your customers?

▶ How could you use the structure provided?

▶ Do you make sure that your proposals appear tailormade and personal?

▶ How could you improve your proposal design?

## How to use this information

Create a simple system for creating winning proposals and getting them done on time.

> **Think winning proposal and increase your**
> **likelihood of getting the business**

# 71 Following up and following through

## What is follow up?

Follow up is carried out by telephone or email after an initial contact has been made with a prospective customer. You may need to follow up the following.

- Leads generated at networking events or conferences.
- Leads or contacts made at talks.
- Sales letters or direct mail.
- Sales proposals.
- Offers on your products and services made to your best customers.
- Research or testing of new ideas.

## Why is follow up important?

Following up sales letters or direct mail can increase the response you get between 20% and 50%. Follow up in general is vital.

Follow up both acts as a reminder and shows that you are interested. Most people will thank you for following up. Another term for follow up is nurturing. By following up you are nurturing your prospective customers.

## Your challenge

Think about how long it typically takes to finally get a piece of business in your industry. Consider whether or not you would have got it if you hadn't been disciplined with your nurturing. Your challenge will be to get into the routine of doing your follow up. This will involve setting up a system and keeping the focus.

## How to follow up successfully

- If your follow up is by telephone always ask if it is convenient to talk.
- Remind of the last contact.
- Explain the purpose of your call.
- Always have full details of your last contact in front of you.
- Get the details right.
- Use their name.

- Connect with the rapport you had the last time you met or spoke. Find some common ground from the start.
- Be disciplined and carry on until you have a conclusion.
- Don't pester – calling and leaving messages every day is not good practice.
- It is better not to ask for the person to call you back. That way you are in control of when you try again. You may leave a message that you called and find out the best time to call back to catch the person in.
- Keep an up-to-date customer management system.

**How GOOD IS YOUR FOLLOW UP? – SPECIAL RESPONSE CHECKLIST**
- How do you handle the follow up of your sales proposals?
- How do you handle the follow up of the contacts you make?
- And sales leads – how many 'Nos' do you get before you give up?
- How much business could you be missing out on by not following up?
- What about following up sales letters or direct mail, have you ever tried it?
- How could you improve your follow up and follow through?
- What impact could this potentially have on your business?

## How to use this information

If you can see the value of follow up and want to test out the impact it could have on your business, set yourself some goals and targets.

*Think follow up and get the business that others miss out on*

14

# Completing your marketing plan

**inspiring ways
to market
your small business**

# 72 Setting your sales and marketing goals

## What is a goal?

A goal is a written statement of intent. It represents an important target that you are aiming for. Your sales and marketing goals will include financial goals such as revenue, profit and income and non-financial goals such as products sold, new customers acquired, contracts signed, articles published, talks delivered, leads generated.

There is more commitment behind a written goal than there is with one which remains as a thought in your head. The level of commitment you make to each goal influences the energy needed to make it happen.

## Why are goals important?

Knowing the mountain you are climbing, and what you want the view to be like when you get to the top, is important to think about before you start to prepare for the trip. Having a destination to go for creates direction and focus.

Clear sales and marketing goals that both you and your team create and commit to are a vital step to a successful marketing plan.

## Your challenge

Your challenge will be to make sure that the goals which you create are SMART. SMART is a simple way of creating goals that are meaningful to you. Your goals must be specific, measurable, achievable, relevant and time bound. If they are woolly, unachievable and completely irrelevant to your vision for the future then it is pointless creating them in the first place. So your first challenge will be to make sure that your goals pass the SMART test.

## How to make your goals SMART

### Specific

- What is the goal/target specifically?
- Write it as if you have already achieved it.

## *Measurable*

- How will you know you have achieved your goal?
- What will have happened or be happening?
- How will you measure the results?

You will need to have something tangible that proves your results.

## *Achievable*

- Is this goal something that is within your own or your team's capability?
- What resources do you have/need to make it happen?
- Do you believe that is it possible?

## *Relevant*

- How is this goal relevant to your vision for your business?

## *Time bound*

- When do you want to achieve it by?
- When can it be achieved?

> **SETTING YOUR OWN SALES AND MARKETING GOALS – SPECIAL RESPONSE CHECKLIST**
> ▶ Look back over your business vision.
> ▶ Remind yourself of some of the things you want to achieve with your marketing.
> ▶ Create some broad sales and marketing goals to give you some direction and focus to start with.
> ▶ Now break these broad areas down into some key areas – sales revenue, generating new customers, building business with existing customers, profile building, website marketing.
> ▶ Consider the sales and marketing goals you have for each section.
> ▶ Write them down – are they SMART?
> ▶ Can you break any of them down into specific targets?

## *Put these goals to the SMART test*

*Sales goals*

- To reach a total revenue of £250,000 by the end of the next financial year.

- To achieve a profit level of 70%.

### New customers

- Ten new customers spending £3,000 per annum by December 2007.
- Five new customers spending £300 per month.

### Existing customer

- To retain 75% of our existing customer base.
- To increase the spend of 50% of our existing customer base by 10%.

### Profile building

- To build our profile within *x* area by achieving five publications regularly publishing our articles.
- To achieve three new poster and billboard sites.
- To create an opportunity to appear on local TV or radio during 2007.

### Website marketing

- To complete our new site by *x* date.
- To set up a Google advert campaign by *x* date.
- To complete our search engine submission package by *x* date.
- To research quality links for our site by *x* date.
- To achieve ten quality website links.

## How to use this information

Once you have set your goals you will need to create a process for ensuring that they stay at the forefront of both your own and your team's mind. You may have them displayed in your office and talked about and reviewed at meetings. You will need to do whatever it takes to keep the focus. A goal will not miraculously happen as a result of creating it in the first place. It is like a seed – to grow it needs to be fed and watered. You will need to take appropriate action to make it happen.

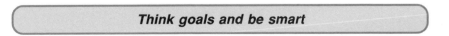

**Think goals and be smart**

# 73 Developing a budget

## What is a budget?

A budget is the amount you estimate spending on your business marketing over a defined period of time. A budget is the amount required to support the resources you will need to achieve the goals you have set. Your budget must balance with your estimated sales revenue figures. It must be an amount that assists in moving your business forward but doesn't bankrupt you in the process. Your marketing budget may be one of many budgets that you set for your business.

## Why is it important?

Having a budget will ensure that you keep on track with the marketing activities that you have planned. Having carefully analysed what the best methods to market your business are, and set some clearly defined goals, you will have created the basis from which you can create your budget. Having a budget will make you stop and think when you get offered new marketing opportunities during the course of the year. You may find yourself having to decline to some late-space advertising because it does not fit into your budget. It will make you more careful and discerning when it comes to making decisions about how you spend your money. This is a good thing, as a lot of money can be wasted with ill-planned, haphazard marketing activities.

## Your challenge

Your biggest challenge will be in accurately setting your budget and then sticking to it. You will need to spend some time working out what resources you will need to make your goals happen. Creating a budget is not about picking a random figure and sticking with it, nor is it as simple as working out what you spent last year and adding 10% for good measure.

## How to create a marketing budget

Your budget can be created in several ways depending on how exact you want to be. You can estimate, or work out an exact figure.

*How to estimate*

If you have been in business for over a year and have been tracking your marketing-related expenditure then you will be able to calculate how much it costs you to acquire one new customer, or costs to sell one product. All you need to do is total up how much you have spent and how many new customers you have acquired or how many units of your product you have sold. Once you have these two figures, simply divide expenditure by either new customers or units sold. This will give you the cost to acquire one customer or sell one unit.

Now take the goals you have set for customer acquisition or unit sales target and multiply them by the unit cost of acquisition. This will give you a rough estimate of what you may need to invest to achieve your goals for next year.

## How to work out an exact figure

This will involve some research on your part. You will have to work out exactly what resources you will need to achieve your sales and marketing goals and what these resources are likely to cost you.

Your list may include all the marketing methods you have decided have the best chance of giving you the greatest return.

Once you have an exact figure you will need to compare it with the revenue that you are planning to achieve over the next 12 months. Your marketing budget should end up as a realistic percentage of the amount you hope to bring into the business.

Marketing is a business expense that whilst being tax deductible still must be set up to bring in a measurable return.

**DEVELOPING YOUR BUDGET – SPECIAL RESPONSE CHECKLIST**
- ▶ Which marketing methods have you chosen to implement?
- ▶ What is it going to cost to utilise your chosen marketing methods?
- ▶ What resources are going to be required to implement these methods?
- ▶ What will you need to invest in each segment to achieve your goals?
- ▶ What return would you expect?
- ▶ How will you measure the return on your investment?

## *How to use this information*

If you haven't set a budget before, then this may be this the time to start. If you have, then perhaps there are ways in which you could improve the process you use. What should you be spending? This is a question that many people ask when they are new to marketing their business. The answer depends very much on what you are planning to achieve and the best route to that. If your marketing spend brings you a good return, then it is an investment not simply expenditure. The more you gain, the more you will be comfortable spending.

> **Think budget and spend wisely**

# 74 Planning your strategy

## What is a strategy?

Your strategy is a description of exactly how you plan to achieve each goal you have set. It is your route map to the end result you have committed to. Your strategy is how you are going to make it happen.

## Why is having one important?

Setting time aside to create a strategy will ensure that you think about and plan your way forward. If you do not do this all you will have is a set of goals and no methodology.

## Your challenge

Allowing yourself time to work *on* your business as opposed to *in* it is your challenge. There will always be something urgent and important to do. Strategy planning is a non-urgent but vitally important task that you must allocate the time to do. You will need to stop doing, start thinking and planning.

## How to create a strategy

You will need a strategy for each of your marketing goals.

---

**Example 1 – Build a strong profile in the Thames Valley Region**

Each mini goal will need a strategy of its own and will need to be broken down into a critical path plan.

|  | 3 | 6 | 9 | 12 |
|---|---|---|---|---|
| NOW → | months → | months → | months → | months |
| ...... | ..... | ..... | ..... | ..... |

Draw a line which represents the length of time it will take to reach the goal.

---

Break that time period down into suitable sections. Create a specific goal for each section of time (these are stepping stones to the final destination).

For each goal in each section you will need to check out the following:

- What needs to happen to achieve this goal?
- What is vital to achieve before you will be able to move on?
- What needs to happen by when?
- How long will things take?
- What resources do you need?
- What resources have you got?

Now plan your steps in their critical order.

**Example 2 – To create the opportunity to speak at one networking event per month**

- Research the different networking events in the Thames Valley.
- Check the fit with ideal target customers.
- Find out about speaking opportunities, requirements and available slots.
- Visit events as a guest.
- Short-list the best.
- Create a brief for a set of hot topics with audience appeal.
- Contact organisers with your offer.
- Plan calendar.
- Create a talk and any supporting promotional material.

This will need to be done for every one of your sales and marketing goals. When you have finished you will have your complete success strategy. It will be a lot easier to plan the days and months ahead once you know exactly what you need to do to make it happen.

### YOUR STRATEGY – SPECIAL RESPONSE CHECKLIST

The following questions will help you to plan your own strategy.

- ▶ How are you going to progress each element of your plan?
- ▶ What is the critical path for each of the goals you have set?
- ▶ What are the milestones and deadlines?
- ▶ What are the steps?
- ▶ What needs setting up?
- ▶ What are the priorities?
- ▶ What specific practical actions need to be taken to make it happen?
- ▶ By whom and by when?
- ▶ How will you monitor, evaluate and review your strategy?

## How to use this information

Take time out to plan your marketing strategy. Involve your team in its creation. Remember, people support that which they help to create.

> **Think strategy and work on your business not just in it**

# 75 Writing the marketing plan

To complete your marketing plan you will need to refer to any notes you may have made as you worked through the individual sections of this book.*

## Why is it important to have a written plan?

This is your opportunity to bring together all the thoughts and ideas you have had about your business marketing. Writing this plan will force you to clarify and articulate these thoughts. Your plan will tell a story about your business and be evidence of all the careful thought you have put into it. You will be able to use this plan to stay focused and on track. Writing a plan creates something tangible that you have committed to. It will be your success blueprint.

## Your plan template

The important headings for your marketing plan can be found on page 8 of this book.

## How to use this information

Take this template and write each section for your business. The relevant chapters in this book will explain exactly what you need to consider. When it is completed it will need to be reviewed and fine tuned. This is not a plan that is cast in stone, it will need to be fluid – moving and adapting to the way your business and your market grows and develops. Your marketing plan gives you the structure, and your strategy, once implemented, gives you the feedback.

> **Think marketing plan and get results**

*If you would like an electronic copy of this template to use to write your plan please go to our resources section at *www.marketingco.biz* or for a editable version email *Jackie@marketingco.biz*

# 15

# The simple things that make a big difference

**inspiring ways
to market
your small business**

# 76 Making it easy for people to buy from you

Ideally you want everyone in your business, everything your business does, everything you stand for, to provide an enjoyable, pleasant and easy experience for your customer.

## Why is this important?

Everybody is busy, and the increased pressure that new technology brings means everything is expected more quickly and instantly. If something doesn't hit between the eyes within the first few seconds of coming into contact, many just do not want to make the effort to try harder to understand, appreciate and use. Instant, positive communication is vital in any industry.

The easier it is to do business with you, the more business you are likely to do. The more difficult, the more business you risk losing. So, how easy and how much fun is it to do business with you?

## Your challenge

Your challenge will be to keep a perspective on your business which enables you to keep seeing it through your customers' eyes. It is easy to get so wrapped up in the detail of the day-to-day running of your business that taking a step back becomes difficult. You need to keep on asking the question 'How can we make it even easier for people to buy from us?'

## How to make it easy to buy

- Make sure that it is obvious what you are selling – you know, but do your customers?

- Ensure that those selling your products or services know and can communicate the value of your products and services.

- Use customer-friendly language – watch jargon and too much detail.

- Avoid giving your customers too much choice, it can be overwhelming.

- Have clear signage inside and outside of your business.

- Keep paperwork to the minimum.

- Shorten the steps in your sales process.

- Design a website that is easy to navigate.

- Make sure there is always easy access to all the information needed to make purchasing decisions.

- Ensure that all your promotional materials have full and obvious contact details.

- If you send prospective customers location maps make sure that they are easy to read and follow.

- Keep your customers informed simply and clearly.

### IS IT EASY TO BUY FROM YOU? – SPECIAL RESPONSE CHECKLIST

▶ How easy is it for your target market to find out about what you do?

▶ Your business name – is it memorable; is it easy for potential customers to make a clear association with the services you offer?

▶ How easy is it for people to find out where you are?

▶ If you have a website, how appealing is it?

▶ How easy is it for people to get the information they need and make contact with you?

▶ Is there any customer education necessary with buying and using your products? If so how easy is it to understand?

▶ What about the structure of your client meetings and appointments – is it easy for people to see clearly how they could benefit from a relationship with you?

▶ What about your business proposals? What do they look like – are they appealing? Is it easy for a customer to assimilate the information?

▶ What about your email or website address. Is it easily memorable?

## How to use this information

Go through every single business communication and buying process that you have set up for your customers. Check them out from the position of actually being a customer. Note your complete experience from start to finish. Learn from it and make any changes you need to make their buying experience easier.

**Think make it easy to buy and increase sales**

# 77 Keeping customers happy

## Why is this important?

If your customers are happy with you and the services that you provide they will remain loyal and keep buying from you. You will be first on their supplier list. They will also happily recommend or refer your services to others. The happier you can keep your customers, the more likely it is that they will buy more from you. They are also less likely to stop buying from you for no very good reason. Price rises will affect a happy customer less because they appreciate the value they receive from you.

## Your challenge

When you make your first sale you may make an extra special effort to communicate to your customer the value they are receiving. This extra special effort may stop once that person becomes a longer-term customer, with you assuming that they know about the value they receive and could receive from you. This may not be the case. People's needs and desires change, they forget, they get offered other options by competitors, they change their mind and they can get buyer's remorse. Your challenge will be to make sure that your customers remain in a happy state of mind about your business whether they are buying or not.

## How to keep customers happy

Keeping customers happy requires a long term communication strategy that includes some of the actions described in previous chapters. Here are some additional quick and easy success tips.

■ Always thank them for their business.

■ Remember something personal about them.

■ Make an effort to remember their name.

■ Give away ideas and help.

■ Do something extra special for them from time to time – send them a relevant article that relates to their business, a book that you think will help them with something they are struggling with, information about some equipment or facilities that they are looking for.

- Remember your top customers' birthdays – set your calendar up to remind you and give them a call on their birthday.

- Send Christmas and other special day cards.

- Remind your customers about the wise decision they made buying from you by reinforcing the value they get post-sale.

- Make sure that you keep the channels of communication open between you and your customer base and regularly ask for their feedback.

- Keep them informed about new products and services and any changes to your operation which may affect them.

### ARE YOUR CUSTOMERS HAPPY? – SPECIAL RESPONSE CHECKLIST

- How do you measure the level of happiness your customers have?
- How many inactive customers do you have?
- How many customers have stopped buying from you?
- How do you get customer feedback year on year?
- How do you ensure that your customers remember the value they receive from you after they have made their first purchase?
- How many of your customers' names do you remember?
- What could you send your special customers in the post to surprise and delight them?

## How to use this information

When I work with a client I find I start noticing articles in newspapers or magazines that are relevant to them. All I do is photocopy it and put it in the post with a short note. I am sure it makes them smile.

One of the reasons for writing this book was to have something of value to give my customers that would keep them happily thinking of me at the same time as getting some good ideas.

There are lots of ways you can use this information. Start thinking about how you can increase the level of happiness your customers have and watch your business grow in direct proportion.

> **Think customer happiness and grow**

## What is a complaint?

A complaint is an expression of customer dissatisfaction. It can be easy to drive customers away if their complaints are ignored or handled badly. A complaint is a statement about expectations that have not been met. A complaint can be a gift if you choose to see it that way.

## Why is getting complaints important?

Your clients and customers have two options when they feel dissatisfied. They can talk or they can just walk away. If they just walk away you have no opportunity to solve the problem, you don't even know what it is. Many people don't complain even though they are unhappy with something. Their reasons can include not wanting to bother anyone or cause a fuss, risking confrontation, or they simply don't know how to. They will probably only express their complaint to other people, one in five people tell up to 20 others. One complaint can turn into negative marketing very quickly.

If you get told about a complaint, it gives you the opportunity to learn about your business, to keep the customer who has complained and ensure that the feedback they give others afterwards about you is positive. If your customers have the courage to complain, it gives you the chance to apologise and put it right. Some customer relationships can be stronger as a result of a complaint being handled well. You can show your customers how much you care about giving them the service they deserve.

Complaints can be one of the best forms of feedback. They can tell you how to improve your product and service. This constant improvement is vital to any business that wants to maintain and grow its market share.

## Your challenge

Your challenge will be to create an atmosphere within your business that encourages customers to complain if they feel that their expectations have not been met. You will need a system for handling them that can immediately deliver the feel-good factor. You and your team will need to listen and put your values into practice – delivering exactly what you promise. In the face of a complaint you and your team will need to remind yourselves of the life-time value of a good customer. Your team will need to be coached in complaint handling and given the authority to provide answers and solutions as quickly as possible. Complaints must be learnt from and the appropriate changes made which prevent them from recurring. Your aim needs be ultimately to reduce the number of complaints that you get.

## How to deal positively with complaints

- Listen, understand exactly what the customer is dissatisfied with and apologise.
- Offer a solution that gives the customer more than they expect and put a smile on their face.

## Examples

If a customer enjoying a meal in a restaurant complains about the main course, offer them a replacement and a free bottle of wine to compensate for their disappointment. If a customer complains about the late delivery of a package they have ordered, thank them for their feedback, do not charge for the delivery and offer free delivery on their next order with you. These are the little extras that make people smile with surprise and are the things that they are more likely to share with others, forgetting the complaint ever happened in the first place.

Write the customer a letter of apology or, better still, as director of the company give them a personal call. There was a story recently about a customer who complained about a problem with a flight he booked through Virgin Atlantic. He got a shock when Richard Branson himself called apologising for the problems and asked the question 'What could we do for you that would ensure you continue to feel good about us?' The result was a first class up grade with a free place for a guest. The customer's day had suddenly improved dramatically.

Let the customer express any negative emotions they might have connected with the complaint without taking it personally. Remember they are complaining about the service not about you. Ask questions to clarify your understanding of the problem and take notes. When the customer feels heard, you will be able to express your appreciation of their feelings and apologise.

Here are some words that will help ensure that the customer feels that his or her frustrations are understood.

'I appreciate that this must have been very frustrating for you. We apologise for the inconvenience that it has caused you. We would like the opportunity to put this right for you immediately.'

Give your customer a choice of solutions. This will give the customer a feeling of being back in control, which is often what they feel has been lost when something goes wrong with their order.

Make sure you and your team keep a complaints log. This complaints log should include: date, customer details, complaint details, cause, solution provided, and – most importantly – system changes to ensure the complaint does not recur.

**YOUR COMPLAINT HANDLING – SPECIAL RESPONSE CHECKLIST**
- How does your business handle complaints?
- What kind of complaints do you tend to get?
- Are there any themes or patterns?
- What have you learnt about how to improve your product or service from the complaints you have had?
- How could you make it easier for customers to express their dissatisfaction if they feel it?
- How do you record customer complaint information?

## How to use this information

Every business from time to time will experience customer dissatisfaction. Nobody is perfect. Mistakes happen. If you and your team see the complaints you get as gifts, do everything possible to learn from them, maintain a positive relationship with the customers who talk, you can only go forward.

> ***Think about a complaint as a gift of learning***

# 79 Motivating your team

## What is a motivated team?

This is a team that has the consistent energy, enthusiasm and focus to make things happen. They share a vision for the future which inspires them. They are committed to the achievement of team goals. They feel important and valued members of the team. They pull together and feel good about what they are doing each and every day. They feel excited to be part of something that is growing and moving forward.

## Why is it important?

The energy and enthusiasm of your team is vital to your productivity and great customer service. A team which feels motivated will give more and achieve more. Their energy is the fuel that is needed to move forward. Your business is only as good as the people who operate within it. In many cases your people are your business. The better they feel, the more likely they are to be efficient, effective and creative. It is in your interest to ensure that you do everything you can to sustain their motivation and commitment. People will work harder and show more loyalty when they feel appreciated and valued for their contribution.

## Your challenge

It can be easy to take your team for granted and to expect them to just do their job because you pay them to do it. Every team will need to be inspired by their leader.

Handing out a Christmas bonus is a nice gesture but it is not enough to sustain long-term motivation. Your team will be affected by the way you communicate your expectations to them. Your challenge will be to consider what you can do to ensure that you create a team atmosphere that is a pleasure to be part of.

## How to motivate your team

- Take time to communicate your vision for the business to them.
- Emphasise the importance of their role.
- Involve the team in your planning process – remember people support that which they help to create.
- Help them to set meaningful goals and objectives.

- Praise their hard work and achievement.
- Hold regular short meetings which keep the focus and recognise success.
- Recognise and reward results.
- Provide an opportunity for some healthy competition.
- Thank individuals for their contribution regularly.
- Smile.
- Organise the occasional team social and have fun.
- Provide learning opportunities.
- Care.

### HOW MOTIVATED IS YOUR TEAM? – SPECIAL RESPONSE CHECKLIST

- ▶ How would you rate the level of motivation your team has?
- ▶ How do you know when they are motivated? What do you notice?
- ▶ How do you know when they are demotivated?
- ▶ What impact does the motivation of your team have on your monthly results?
- ▶ What could you do differently to add spark to your team's energy and enthusiasm?
- ▶ What about arranging a team day or evening out? What could you do?

## *How to use this information*

As the business owner you may be the natural team leader. Be aware of the impact of your leadership style on the team. Is your behaviour inspiring or not? You do have an influence over your team's different levels of motivation and there is a lot you can do to make a difference.

> ***Think team and harness its power and energy***

# 16

# Creating a marketing system

**inspiring ways
to market
your small business**

## 80 Keeping customer records

### What is a customer record?

Customer records contain important information vital to maintaining an ongoing relationship with your customers. These records will contain customers' full name, company name, address, telephone, mobile, fax, email, website, birthday, business information, work/client history, samples of work, personal information (as appropriate) and spending patterns.

Customer records can be stored on a database or customer relationship management (CRM) system. There are many good CRM systems on the market today which will enable you to store, access and manage your contacts and communicate with these customers.

### Why is this important?

Your customers are your business. Your existing customers form the bedrock providing the foundation from which to grow. Your prospects are your future. The only way you are going to be able to build your relationship with these people is to communicate with them. If you are to do that effectively then you will need a system. Any system starts with customer records. Names written on scraps of paper, held in your head or contained in your inbox is not an effective way to manage your database. It can be extremely time-consuming to operate in this way and you will end up continually chasing your tail. If you have full and detailed customer records you will be able to understand your business better. You will be able to analyse spending patterns and see trends. This information can help you with your future business decisions and marketing activities.

### Your challenge

Your challenge will be firstly in choosing and setting up a customer database or CRM system that suits your needs, and secondly in maintaining the discipline required to capture, store and update your customers' details.

### How to get your customer details

Depending on how you normally take customer orders you will need to make sure that you and your team develop an easy way of getting all the information you need at the same time. When a person becomes a new customer they expect to be asked for their details. They have made a decision to buy and at that moment are likely to feel the greatest connection. They could be interested in the potential value of being kept informed, supported and in touch by the company that they have just done business with.

- Ask for full customer details at the point of sale.

- Get into the habit of doing this and create a system that works and doesn't take the customer too much time.

- Take electronic details if you can – if not write in capitals.

- Make sure you give them a good reason for taking their details.

- Make sure everything is spelt correctly.

- Make sure your customers are called at least once a year and their details updated. This provides another valuable communication opportunity.

- Make sure whoever is responsible for keeping the customer records up to date does it religiously. It is much easier to do it day by day than it is to leave it, let it build up and risk losing information.

**HOW GOOD ARE YOUR CUSTOMER RECORDS? – SPECIAL RESPONSE CHECKLIST**
- How do you keep customer records?
- Is the system you use user-friendly?
- How up to date are your current records?
- Do your records contain all the information you need?
- What additional information do you need?
- How often do your records get updated?
- What could you do to improve your customer record keeping?

## How to use this information

Every customer you get has a life-time value. That life-time value will only be fulfilled if they are kept happy, contented and communicated with. Use this information to prompt an honest appraisal of your current customer record system. Do what it takes to make your system work in the best way possible.

> *Think customer records and make constant contact easier*

# 81 Building an opt-in mailing list

## What is an opt-in mailing list?

An opt-in list is a list of contacts that you have built yourself. It will contain the names, addresses and contact details of people that have agreed or asked to be contacted by you. They will be the people who have ticked a box on one of your website forms saying that they would like to receive a free monthly newsletter, a free report, regular product update or special promotion. They may have handed you a business card at a networking event and asked to receive your information.

## Why is this important?

Building your own list has several advantages. You will know that every name you have on that list is someone who has demonstrated that they have an interest in what you do. When you communicate with them they are more likely to pay attention to what you send them because they asked for it. You can also be confident that the names, addresses and telephone numbers are up to date.

If a person has put their hand up and said 'Yes I want to be contacted by you,' they are one step closer to becoming a customer of yours. It is much more cost effective to communicate with a list of people who are potentially hungry for what you are offering than it is to do the same with those you only suspect might be interested.

Buying or renting direct mailing or email mailing lists can mean that a lot of your mail goes in the bin and your emails become irritating spam. This is a terrible waste of your time, money and effort. Creating your own opt-in list will enable your marketing to be much more targeted.

## Your challenge

Your challenge will be to put the right bait in front of the right people to attract them to opt-in to your list. People will only say yes if they think that they are going to get something of value as a result. Firstly you will have to find out where the people are that are likely to be interested in your product or service. Secondly work out what it is that would draw them to you. Thirdly go fishing with your tasty bait. Creating an opt-in list that is full of the right people will require a well thought-out and carefully planned strategy.

## *How to create your list*

- Give people a compelling reason to say 'I want more'.

- Create a free report, offer a free sample, a free newsletter, a free heath check, a free consultation connected with your service that is exactly what people need.

> **Here are some examples**
> A nutritionist offers a free report called 'How to feel super charged' along with a free health report.
>
> A financial consultant offers a free report called 'How to raise finance for your business venture' and a free financial assessment.
>
> A property company offers free monthly property industry update with buying and selling tips and advice.
>
> A professional association offers a free newsletter that contains valuable up-to-date market and business research data.

- Develop a title for your newsletter or free report that promises a benefit and suggests important learning. You can then use this along with your message asking interested people to respond. The title should sell the value and motivate action. Here are two examples of the lead generation messages I use for Marketingco.

> **Do you need a marketing plan for your business?**
> Get your *free* report now
> Eight steps to profit making marketing plan
> email *Jackie@marketingco.biz*
>
> Or
>
> **Do you want a constant flow of marketing ideas?**
> Get our *free* monthly newsletter
> Money Making Marketing Ideas
> email *Jackie@marketingco.biz*

■ You will need to put these lead generation messages in places where your 'hungry crowd' are most likely to be. Find out all the places your target customer goes, takes part in and reads.

■ Make a list of the best places to post your message. This could be professional association newsletters and magazines, networking groups' websites, business club forums, chat rooms, online discussion groups, newspapers and specialist magazines, Google adverts, classified advertising in targeted complimentary business e-zines.

■ Some business clubs or groups will allow members to make special member offers. This is a good opportunity to promote your free offer.

■ You can offer a free tip to an e-zine that targets your market in return for promoting your free newsletter or report.

■ You can offer free ideas and advice to anyone asking questions about your area of expertise on online discussion forums.

■ You can promote your free newsletter and your free reports on your website.

### CREATING YOUR OWN LIST – SPECIAL RESPONSE CHECKLIST

▶ What could you offer as bait to attract your own hungry crowd to become part of your list?

▶ What do you know that your hungry crowd are interested in?

▶ How could you get some feedback and find out?

▶ What could you call your free newsletter, report or offer that would sell it to your target customer?

▶ Where could you promote it?

▶ How many people would you like to get onto your list?

## How to use this information

Building a list is the best way to ensure a solid foundation from which to grow your business. Once you have a list you will have created a very warm market for what you do. So it is worth studying this information and considering exactly how you can implement these strategies to build your biggest and best list.

> **Think list...and build your business**

# 82 Creating a communication calendar

## What is a communication calendar?

A communication calendar is your plan for all the individual marketing touches you intend to make over the course of any 12-month period. It is a complete schedule of events and activities. A communication calendar is your record of all the different ways which you are going to stay in touch with your customers. It could be through email marketing, e-zine, newsletter, information updates, telecommunication, website promotions, Christmas or other special day cards, invitations to social events, free talks, direct mail promotions and more.

## Why is this important?

Keeping in touch with your customers is about keeping your customers in the loop. It is about reminding them that you care about their interests and needs. Having a calendar that plots each keep-in-touch activity will make planning easier. You can analyse the flow of touches from the customers' point of view and ask yourself important questions like

- Is it enough?
- Is it too much?
- Are the activities the right ones, in the right order?

## Your challenge

Your challenge will be to create a calendar that offers exactly the right amount of touches. The right amount of communication is subtle, as it must neither be too much nor too little. Your customers will not want to be bombarded with information from you. In previous chapters each communication method will have been covered in more depth. Know what you want to achieve and then design your calendar of activities to suit.

## How to create a communication calendar

Each part of your plan should ultimately fit together like the pieces of a jigsaw puzzle. Each element can support and link to each other.

Your electronic newsletter can be used to deliver useful information as well as to promote an aspect of your business that your customer will find of value. The promotion that you choose can then be linked to your website and links provided in the newsletter to encourage traffic. Telephone calls to update customer records can be linked to invitations to events or customer needs reviews. Direct mail and email updates can be run concurrently, enabling one to support the other.

You may choose to have different communication calendars for your existing customers and for those prospects who have opted in to receive communication from you, but have not yet become customers. You may also have special communication calendars for individual clients that you are nurturing.

## Sample calendar

This is a sample calendar that could be used for existing customers and elements of it for new prospects.

| | |
|---|---|
| **January** | Happy New Year Newsletter – sale – website promotion |
| **February** | Newsletter – new products update |
| **March** | Newsletter – special Easter promotion – website promotion |
| **April** | Newsletter – telecommunication customer record update |
| **May** | Newsletter – annual customer review – website promotion |
| **June** | Newsletter – conference email/direct mail |
| **July** | Newsletter – special hospitality event – website promotion |
| **August** | Newsletter – conference email/direct mail |
| **September** | Newsletter – telecommunication – website promotion |
| **October** | Newsletter – conference – customer satisfaction survey |
| **November** | Newsletter – Christmas gift ideas email – website promotion |
| **December** | Newsletter – Christmas card – Christmas party |

**YOUR OWN CALENDAR – YOUR SPECIAL RESPONSE CHECKLIST**
▶ What do you want your communication calendar to achieve?
▶ What methods are you going to use to touch your customers over a 12-month period?
▶ How are you going to ensure each touch supports and links with the other?
▶ What are you going to use each touch for?
▶ Make a plan and check out what it looks like.
▶ Consider what you are planning from the customers' point of view.

▶ Get some feedback from your team.

▶ How are you going to implement this plan?

## How to use this information

A communication calendar is an excellent way to ensure you plan and deliver your keep-in-touch marketing on time and on schedule. Study this information and use it to motivate yourself to create your own. Measure the results it brings you over the 12-month period.

> **Think communication calendar and get constant attention**

# Making it happen

**inspiring ways
to market
your small business**

# 83 Fine tuning your plan

## *What does this mean?*

Fine tuning your plan means evaluating its success year on year and making the changes required to continue to succeed with it. Your marketing plan will be tailor-made by you to achieve your goals and objectives. Ideally you will create a new updated marketing plan each year.

## *Why is it important?*

Twelve months is a long time and you may find that things change. Your original plans will need fine tuning to work alongside any new or additional priorities. The plan you have created will provide you with a solid and well-considered structure. This may need some flexibility, a contingency fund, or the benefit of trial and error to get it absolutely right.

As you start to implement your plan it will become live and active in the real world. That is where the real learning will begin.

## *Your challenge*

This may be the first time that you have ever given so much thought to a marketing plan for your business. It may be the one and only time you have articulated and written down all the ideas that you have had in your head for many years. It may have required an effort to do this. Once something of this nature is complete it can be easy to think 'that's it now I'm done'. If only it were that simple. Just as the seasons change the needs and desires of your marketplace will too. You will also change how you think and the ideas you have today will have developed further in the months and years ahead. Nothing stands still, and especially not your marketing plan.

## *How to fine tune your plan*

As you will be actioning your plan week by week and month by month you will get the opportunity to test out some of your strategies. As you see how well they work you may fine tune as you go. Your marketing plan is your working structure that needs to be referred to from time to time. It should not be kept in a drawer out of sight otherwise it will be forgotten. Holding a regular, monthly marketing meeting is a useful way of creating an opportunity to review what is being implemented on a regular basis. Give the meeting a structure that keeps you focused on the key elements of your plan. This meeting can be with everybody who is involved with the marketing of your business.

## Sample marketing meeting structure

- Highlights of the month.
- What marketing activities have we implemented this month?
- How well have they worked – what is our evidence?
- What could we fine tune or improve?
- What have we got planned for next month?
- Allocation of tasks and responsibilities.
- Marketing goals.
- Action plan for the month.

**YOUR SPECIAL RESPONSE CHECKLIST**
- ▶ How well is the plan working?
- ▶ Are we using our resources wisely?
- ▶ What if anything is likely to affect this plan over the next 12 months?
- ▶ What else do we need to consider or add to the plan?

## How to use this information

See your plan as a live working document and keep it close to you. Creating a marketing plan should become an annual discipline. It will ensure that you keep committed to the important thought process that is vital to enabling the creation of a profit-making, not a loss-making, marketing plan.

> **Think fine tune and stay ahead**

# 84 Maintaining awareness and learning from experience

## What does this mean?

Maintaining awareness is about keeping your eyes and ears open and knowing what is going on in your business. It is about being open to feedback, being able to take a step back from time to time and see what is happening. It is about recognising what is needed to move forward. Learning from experience will allow you to stop doing things that are obviously not working quickly and easily.

## Why Is it important?

Maintaining awareness is vital to the ongoing success of your business marketing. Continuous learning allows you and your business to grow. In a world that is continually changing and with greater and greater pressure to be better, faster and slicker, if you are not learning and moving with the times, you will soon get left behind. Your eyes and ears must be open and alert; you cannot afford to assume anything will continue in the same way indefinitely.

## Your challenge

From experience I know that it can be easy to get so close to your business and so involved in the day-to-day pressures that it can be hard to take that important step back and evaluate what is going on. Time seems to fly by and before you know it another year has passed by. If you don't stop and give yourself time to think, you run the danger of your business running you. Great marketing takes great thinking, and you can't do that on the run from one thing to another and back again. Don't get stuck in the loop of repeatedly talking about what you don't want to happen whilst continuing in the same old ways.

Remember the definition of madness: 'Doing the same thing whilst wanting a different result'.

Change happens when you take action to get what you want. This may mean that you have to shake off the old habits and create some new ones. You will need habits that can support you in getting the fulfilling business life and results you deserve.

## *How to maintain awareness*

Everything you do you can learn from. What works and what doesn't are the two questions that you need to keep asking yourself and your team. Keep your senses alive and see your marketing activities through your customers' eyes as well as your own. Listen to the feedback you are getting. Notice the way the people who matter to you and your business are responding to everything that you do. Stay sharp and alert. Do not allow yourself to return to old habits and comfortable familiar routines.

**YOUR SPECIAL RESPONSE CHECKLIST**
- ▶ What can I learn from my experiences today?
- ▶ What am I more aware of now that I wasn't before?
- ▶ What do I really want to change?
- ▶ What am I doing about it?
- ▶ What is my evidence that things are changing?
- ▶ What is good about what is happening?

## *How to use this information*

Keep questioning yourself. The right questions will stimulate your mind and ensure that you train your brain to look for the answers you need to move forward. Stay alert and feed your mind with what it needs to succeed.

> **Think be aware and keep your senses alive**

# 85 Staying on track

## What does this mean?

Staying on track means paying attention to your goals and your plans and making sure that you and your team are taking those important daily steps forward. Don't give up when it is tough or something doesn't work first time round.

## Why is it important?

**Marketing works if you work at it** . . . and that is what it takes. There may not be one single miracle that will turn everything around, however there will be a series of simple, practical ideas that, once implemented, will ensure you get those important results.

The magic starts to happen when you stay on track and do what it takes to make it happen. You need to get really good at marketing your business. It is well worth making the effort. The better you are at marketing the quicker you will **grow** your business.

## Your challenge

It can be easy to feel motivated and inspired after reading a book like this, attending a seminar or after seeing some good initial results from your marketing efforts. The hard work will be in staying on top and feeling the energy each day from now on.

## How to stay on track

Question yourself and then try another way. Very few of us get it completely right first time round. Hold regular review meetings and talk about your successes as well as what else you could improve. Read and re-read this book. It will always stimulate a new way of looking at something, prompt action and inspire you all over again.

**STAYING ON TRACK – YOUR SPECIAL RESPONSE CHECKLIST**

▶ Ask yourself and your team from time to time – how are we doing?

▶ What is working well and what isn't?

▶ How could we improve?

▶ What could we do more of to make a difference?

▶ What have we done really well?

▶ What are we most proud off?

▶ Do I need to read this book again?

## *How to use this information*

Your attitude to making it happen will be the key to your success. Be determined to make it work for you. Stop haphazard marketing activities and the time, effort and money that you waste when it doesn't work as well as it could. Start thinking about what you are doing and planning your approach. It really will be worth it in the long term when you finally reap the rewards that you deserve.

> **Think – Am I on track right now?**

Good luck and I wish you all success and happiness that using these ideas brings you.